Enjoying your Jaguar in England

Published by
KELSEY PUBLISHING LTD

Printed in Singapore by Stamford Press PTE Ltd.
on behalf of
Kelsey Publishing Ltd,
Cudham Tithe Barn,
Berry's Hill,
Cudham,
Kent TN16 3AG
Tel: 01959 541444
Fax: 01959 541400
E-mail: kelseybooks@kelsey.co.uk

© 2002

ISBN: 1 873098 60 X

Front Cover:
3.2-litre X300. On the outskirts of the town of Thaxted in Essex.

Contents

Cotswolds 4

Cirencester to Chipping Campden 10

Kent 16

Yorkshire Dales 22

North Yorkshire Dales 28

Hampshire 34

North Essex & South Suffolk 41

West Country 46

Thames Valley 52

Derbyshire Peak District 60

Introduction

Driving is something I have always had a passion for, and am fortunate in having a wife who, for nearly 30 years, has shared that enthusiasm.

It is for this reason, that we have spent many particularly enjoyable hours doing what we call 'bumbling'. Just point the car in any chosen direction and see what you find. If a road is sign posted 'unsuitable for motor vehicles' we invariably drive down it, and have found some real gems as a result. Needless to say, we have also come badly unstuck on a few occasions.

However, the knowledge and experience we have gained over the years, led to us organising and hosting weekend breaks and tours for owners of Jaguar cars, both in the UK and Europe.

From here it seemed a natural progression to write a series of articles entitled 'Enjoying your Jaguar' that have appeared on a regular basis in *Jaguar Monthly* magazine. And it is from that part-work that this book has been produced.

Most of these mini tours can be completed in a day, but can certainly be stretched to make a very enjoyable long weekend.

Whether you chose a days run, or extend it for a couple or more, I hope you will get pleasure from the wonderful scenery this country has to offer, along with stunning villages and outstanding places of interest.

Relax and enjoy your driving.

Jerry Stamper

Enjoying your Jaguar

I have been visiting this particular part of the country for more years than I care to remember, and have had the pleasure of seeing it at its best during all four seasons. The warm summer sun lighting up the honey-coloured Cotswold stone buildings, from the grandest manor house to the smallest and most idyllic cottage; stunning early winter morning scenery dusted with sparkling frost, or blanketed in snow – and let us not forget the fresh colours of early spring, nor the breathtaking reds, browns and golds of a Cotswold Autumn. I have been fortunate enough to see them all.

But where or what precisely are 'The Cotswolds'?

Apart from simply being a range of hills, it is usually accepted that it's an area bounded by Bath in the South, Oxford in the East, Stratford-on-Avon in the North and Malvern in the West.

So you can see it's a pretty extensive area, covering some six counties. It is perhaps best known for its outstandingly attractive villages, but the area has a great deal more to offer the recreational traveller – not least the wide range of accommodation to be found, be it well-run and comfortable bed-and-breakfasts, or internationally renown five star hotels. So, join me for a drive

Bath time

We'll start this particular journey from the spa town of Bath, famous for its splendid architecture, Pump Room and Roman Baths. Maybe you will have spent the previous night staying at Leighton House.

A bed-and-breakfast situated in Wells Road, just a pleasant walk from the city centre, this elegant Victorian house offers excellent accommodation, and the proprietors make their guests feel most welcome. Alternatively, just six miles outside Bath, in the village of Colern, there's the four red star Lucknam Park Hotel, a magnificent Palladian mansion dating from 1720. Set in 500 acres of parkland, the hotel has elegant dayrooms and individually decorated and furnished bedrooms, with high standards of comfort and quality.

Leaving Bath we travel via the A46 and A420 to visit Castle Combe. The village was once voted the prettiest in Britain, and was the location for the filming of *Dr Doolittle*. You'll have to leave your car at the car park, just a short stroll away, but walking down into the village centre the setting is, to my mind, quite breathtaking. Many of the Cotswold stone houses date back to the 15th century, and the church of St Andrews still retains some of its 13th century walls.

Castle Combe boasts two extremely pleasant hotels. The three star *Castle Inn*, whose charm and character have been preserved during recent considerate restoration of its 11 cosy bedrooms. Surrounded by 26 acres of gardens and parkland

Jerry Stamper, Jaguar Monthly's tours manager, reveals some of the UK's most attractive locations. Part One: The Cotswolds - from Bath to Broadway.

The superb XK120 fhc owned by Dieter Adomeit from Germany arrives in the courtyard of the 16th century **Lygon Arms** *coaching inn in Broadway.*

Enjoying Your Jaguar
continued

On the Cotswold escarpment, high above the Vale of Evesham early one frosty December morning.

The unique Pultney Bridge, spanning the river Avon in the Regency town of Bath.

One of the beautifully furnished bedrooms in the Lucknam Park Hotel, near Bath.

Castle Combe village, showing the cosy and comfortable Castle Inn hotel – ideal for an overnight stay or a filling lunchtime snack.

sweeping down to the river Bybrook, the *Manor House* hotel has been awarded four red stars by the AA, and is nothing less than superb. Many of the bedrooms have unique bath and shower rooms, the dining room and extensive lounges have a wonderful relaxed air, and you can't but feel totally at home.

Needless to say, this all comes at a price, but everyone should stay at least one night, just for the experience. The *Manor House* also own the adjacent 18-hole championship golf course, available for the use of guests – it was designed by Peter Allis and is one of the most beautiful in England.

Past a Royal Residence

Tearing ourselves away from this truly delightful spot, we pick up the B4039 heading for Tetbury. On the way we pass Badminton House, famous for the annual Horse Trials (three were found guilty only this year...). Having passed through Little Badminton, take the A433 north east to Tetbury.

Tetbury is an old market town, and is well known as the home of HRH The Prince of Wales, with Highgrove being close by. The town is well worth a visit, for there are a large number of antique dealers and some very attractive architecture. If you're there around lunch time, try the *Snooty Fox* opposite the market square. The food's good and both the bar and dining room of this cosy hotel have a pleasant and relaxed atmosphere. With just 12 very attractive bedrooms, it's quiet too.

Find the A4135 – or, if you are a little more adventurous, the unclassified road which runs parallel – and make your way to Uley. Getting off the main roads you will find some of the most stunning scenery to be found anywhere, particularly around the tiny village of Owlpen. Owlpen Manor is also worth a visit, but check to see that it's open beforehand. Moving on, travel north via the B4066.

It's a steep climb from Uley up towards Nympsfield. When you reach the top, keep an eye open for the picnic sight on the left. The views across the Severn Valley are nothing short of breathtaking.

A very different view

A short distance further on and you'll find the Bristol & Gloucester Gliding Club. For about £45 you can have a trial lesson, and there is no better way of seeing the area. I try to avoid the place as my wife is becoming hooked.

Continuing along the B4066, we drive down into Stroud. Once reckoned to produce the finest broadcloth in the country, it still makes most of the baize for the world's billiard tables. Drive through the town and find the B4070. This will take you up the Slad Valley, with more stunning views. You could do with the relevant Ordinance Survey map at this point, using it to find your way on unclassified roads to Miserden, Edgeworth and most attractive of all, Duntisbourne Leer, where you will have to take your Jaguar for a little paddle. Driving through these tiny hamlets which are well off the usual tourist routes is like stepping back in time.

Now for rather more relaxed driving, going back to A and B roads for the next leg of the journey.

Another well-known Regency town

Having found our way across country, pick up the A435 at Perrott's Brook, turning north along the Churn Valley.

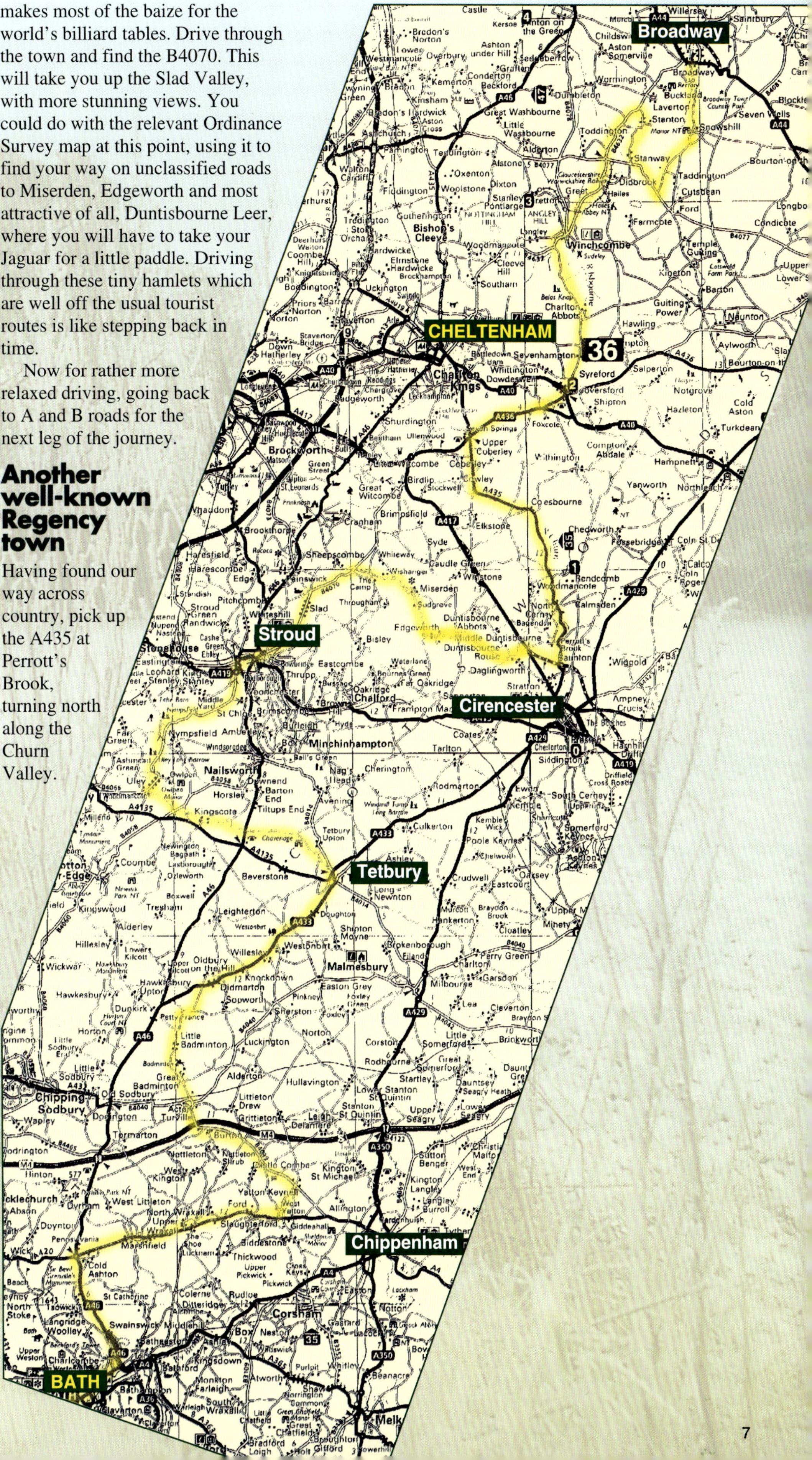

Carol Stamper is securely strapped into a glider at the Bristol & Gloucester Gliding Club prior to a very different view of the Cotswolds.

7

Enjoying Your Jaguar
continued

At Upper Coberley, carry straight on to visit the Spa town of Cheltenham.

Or turn right on the A436. On reaching the A40, turn left and 500yds further on turn right. Again using the OS map, try the country lanes via Brockhampton and Charlton Abbots to Winchcombe. Apart from being a very attractive small town, Winchcombe also contains Sudeley, the medieval castle where Catherine Parr, the last wife of Henry VIII, lived. The castle was reconstructed in 1858 by Sir George Gilbert Scott. The town also has many pubs and tea shops to enjoy, depending on the time of day and your preference of liquid refreshment.

Leaving Winchcombe north on the B4632, you will pass Toddington and the Gloucestershire & Warwickshire Railway. The old station buildings have been renovated, steam trains run to a regular timetable, and you can see the countryside from a different perspective.

A couple of miles north again on the B4632, turn right to Stanton. Driving up to the top of this particularly attractive village, you'll find the *Mount Inn*. This is another good place to stop, but you will need good brakes when leaving the car park.

A little piece of Japan

Try finding your way via Stanway – up the hill, along some single track country lanes – through to Snowshill. Nestled away from the main tourist route, Snowshill is a gem, and Snowshill Manor, owned by the National Trust, is an absolute must for a visit – it contains the lifelong gatherings of the eccentric collector Charles Padget Wade. It includes more than 20 full suits of Samurai armour, along with clocks, toys and musical instruments.

We will conclude this particular journey by following the sign-posts to the well-known Cotswold town of Broadway. The short drive from Snowshill gives wonderful vistas of the Vale of Evesham, famous for the annual crop of asparagus.

Known as 'the show village of England', the broad main street lined with beautiful houses and quaint cottages gives Broadway its name. For an overnight stay, there's the *Broadway Hotel* fronting onto the wide village green. Constructed with a mixture of half timber and Cotswold stone, this three star hotel has both warmth and character. Further up the high street can be found the internationally famous *Lygon Arms*. A five star 16th century coaching inn, both Charles I and Oliver Cromwell stayed there at different times. This hotel offers every comfort and has leisure facilities second to none.

The village itself has a wide range of shops, including art galleries and antique dealers. Window shopping is a favourite pastime for many of its visitors.

That concludes our little tour. Next time we will have a look at the Southern part of this fascinating area of the country, taking in Burford, Northleach and the 'Slaughters'. ●

Jerry Stamper's Lynx D-Type parked outside the charming Broadway Hotel, situated on the village green in Broadway.

Sudely Castle, Winchcombe, home of Catherine Parr, the last wife of Henry VIII.

From Bath to Broadway

Hotels

Lucknam Park	nr. Bath	Four red star / *SP*
Leighton House B&B	Bath	AA Premier Selected
The Manor House	Castle Combe	Four red star / *SP*
The Castle Inn	Castle Combe	Three Star
The Snooty Fox	Tetbury	Three Star
The Broadway Hotel	Broadway	Three Star / *SP*
The Lygon Arms	Broadway	Four red star / *SP*

Places of interest

Roman Baths	Bath
Pump Room	Bath
Abbey Church	Bath
Owlpen Manor	Owlpen
Sudeley Castle	Winchcombe
Gloucestershire & Warwickshire Railway	Toddington
Snowshill Manor	Snowshill

The villages
Castle Combe, Brockhampton, Uley, Winchcombe, Slad, Miserden, Duntisbourne Leer, Stanton, Stanway, Snowshill.

SP = secure parking.

Visit it. Enjoy it. Protect it.

Join the National Trust today and you'll never be far away from a great day out.

As an admirer of Britain's finest cars, you appreciate the importance of taking care of something special. Become a member of Britain's largest conservation charity and you'll not only enjoy free entry to over 300 places of outstanding natural beauty or historical significance, but you'll also be helping us protect them for generations to come.

Protect your heritage. Join the National Trust – from as little as 9p a day.

For more details, call us today on **0870 458 4000**

www.nationaltrust.org.uk

Quoting the reference A511
Registered Charity no. 205846

Top Left: Gribbin Head, Cornwall, NTPL/David Noton *Top centre:* Powis Castle, Powys, NTPL/Andrew Butler *Top Right:* Nymans Garden, Sussex, NTPL/Stephen Robson
Bottom: Baddesley Clinton, Warwickshire, NTPL/Roger Hickman

Enjoying your Jaguar

Jerry Stamper guides us on a tour recommended to get the most relaxing pleasure and enjoyment out of a Jaguar.

Part Two:
Cirencester to Chipping Campden.

In the first part of this series we took a day's drive through just a small part of the western edge of the Cotswolds.

For our second outing, we return to the Cotswolds, but on this occasion we travel through the centre of this most attractive area.

Take more gin with your water

This month's recommended tour starts from the 'capital' of the Cotswolds, Cirencester, which in Roman times was the second largest town in England. But following its decline after the Romans departure, it was the medieval wool trade that put it back on the map.

Indeed it was wool money that paid for the building of the parish church of St John the Baptist, one of the largest Tudor churches of its kind in the country. The town stands at the junction of three Roman roads – The Fosse Way, Ermine Street and Akeman Street – and the most impressive collection of Roman remains is contained in the Corinium museum.

Leaving Cirencester we take the B4425 north west through Barnsley, to visit the village of Bibury. Situated on the river Coln, I never cease to be fascinated by this unique little hamlet. You could stand all day watching the trout almost shoulder to shoulder in the gin-clear water.

Perhaps the most famous part of the village is Arlington Row, a terrace of weavers' cottages fronting onto the river, and now owned by the National Trust. Arlington Mill has become a museum and has an adjoining trout farm.

For an overnight stay in the village, there's the Swan Hotel, a quite delightful 17th century coaching inn. The bedrooms are individually styled and include rooms with four-poster beds. Alternatively, there is the Bibury Court hotel located on the outskirts of the village, where the mood is of peace and tranquillity. There are three golf courses and trout fishing nearby.

Another very pleasant hotel can be found on the outskirts of Bibury, the Bibury Court dates back to 1633.

On the outskirts of Chipping Campden: traditional Cotswold stone with mullion windows but, unusual for this part of the Cotswolds, thatched roofs.

Bright winter sunshine on the River Eye, at Lower Slaughter.

Lower Slaughter, with its 19th century brick mill in the background.

Enjoying your Jaguar
continued

A very popular place during the summer months. The River Windrush flows gently through the village of Bourton-on-the-Water.

Just a mile further up the River Eye from Lower Slaughter, the quaint village of Upper Slaughter.

A magical musical tour

Using secondary roads via the Coln valley, we make our way north to the town of Northleach, which is just off the Roman Fosse Way. Found amongst its stone cottages and almshouses, make a point of visiting Keith Harding's World of Mechanical Music.

For about £4 you will be entertained by the playing of musical instruments, all in the best possible working order. As the name implies, they are all mechanically driven, ranging from the earliest musical boxes to the most sophisticated harmoniums. An experience not to be missed.

Once again, using secondary roads make your way via Farmington, Sherbourne, Windrush and Little Barrington (where I believe you will find the smallest post office in the country) to Burford. The roads are all pretty narrow and will require some care when driving, but the scenery along the Windrush valley is nothing short of superb.

Burford is one of those popular Cotswold towns that can get fairly busy; if you can't find parking on the High Street, there is a large public car park, which is well sign posted.

Another typical wool town, the main street is lined with honey-coloured local stone buildings, and descends a steep hill to cross the River Windrush by a narrow, ancient bridge.

Take your time in the town, as there are many fine shops, and you may wish to stop for morning coffee in one of the attractive pubs or tea shops. If it is lunch time, we usually finish up at the Mermaid Inn, halfway down the hill. The service is efficient and the food and beer first class.

Crossing the old bridge and turning left on the A424, make your way towards the 'Slaughters'.

A pretty muddy place

A very popular tourist spot you may wish to visit is the town of Bourton-on-the-Water. A short distance off the A429, Bourton has a great many attractions, including a model village and the Cotswold Motor Museum. The museum is the home of BRUM, the little car which featured in the children's television series of the same name.

The town, being so popular, can get very busy during the summer months with the grass verge along the river being total obscured by half-naked bodies when the sun shines. So it may be one place you would want to give a miss.

However, during the winter, it's a different story entirely, especially on the lead up to Christmas. A huge Christmas tree covered in plain white lights is always placed on a small island in the middle of the river. At night-time with the reflections in the water, the scene is quite magical.

Returning to the A424, a short distance north, and we turn left into the 'Slaughters'. Lower and Upper Slaughter situated on the River Eye are barely a mile apart, and must be the archetypal examples of a Cotswold village.

Both are a stroller's paradise. The rather grim sounding name which the villages share has nothing to do with death, the word comes from the Anglo-Saxon slohtre, which means nothing more gruesome than 'muddy place'.

A taster for an appetite

From here we drive the short distance to Stow-on-the-Wold. Standing on a ridge between the

Lined with honey-coloured buildings of local stone, the main street of Burford runs down to cross the River Windrush via an ancient bridge.

valleys of the Rivers Windrush and Evenlode, it is the highest hilltop town in the Cotswolds. Hence the local saying, "Stow-on-the-Wold where the wind blows cold".

During the Civil War a battle was fought here in 1646, and hundred of Royalists were imprisoned in the town. Quieter now, the large market square has any number of antique shops, pubs and restaurants, making it the perfect place for a lunch stop.

If you are ready for an overnight halt, then the four-star Wyck Hill House set in 100 acres of woodlands and gardens may be the place for you.

Or there is the excellent Grapevine Hotel in Sheep Street, more convenient for the town centre and its shopping.

Picking up the A429 we continue north to the town of Morton-in-Marsh. A small market town, one of its claims to fame is the interesting old White Hart Inn, where Charles I slept in 1643.

I can thoroughly recommend the Manor House Hotel as a first class spot for lunch. It can be found on the main street, and if the sun's shining the lovely garden is perfect. Try the hot savoury croissants, a bit unforgiving on the waist line, but delicious all the same.

If you take a small detour out of the town along the A44, you'll find the Batsford Arboretum, alongside a centre for Birds of Prey. During the summer months the birds are flown on a regular basis, and you'll have the chance to get a real close-up.

The National Trust at its finest

Returning to the town, we now track cross country on

Owned by the National Trust, Arlington Row in the village of Bibury is made up of these old and attractive weavers' cottages.

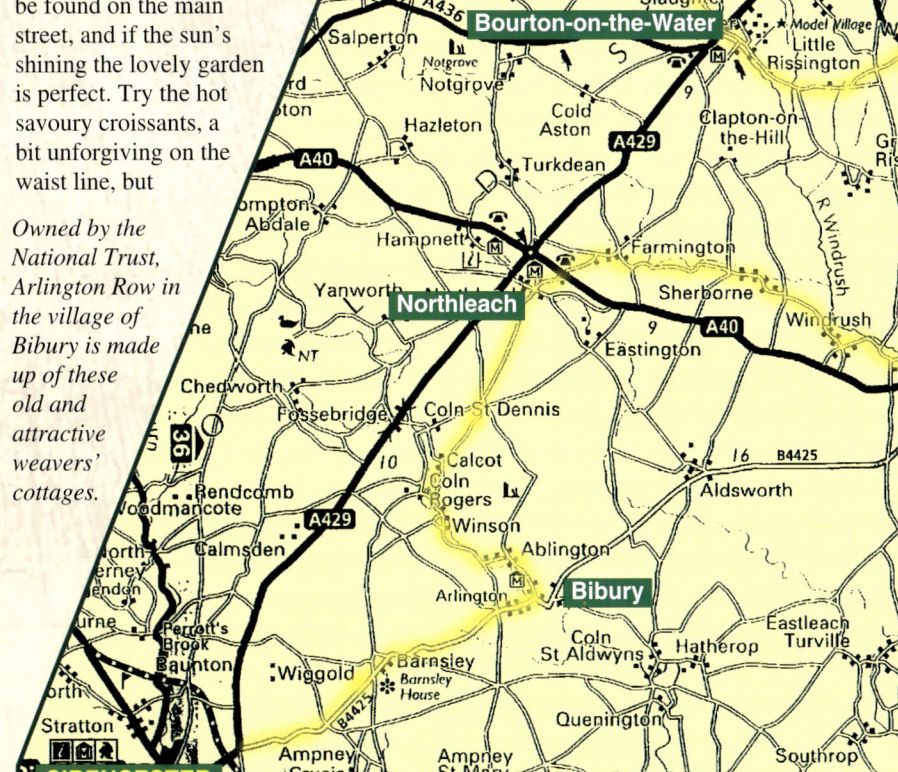

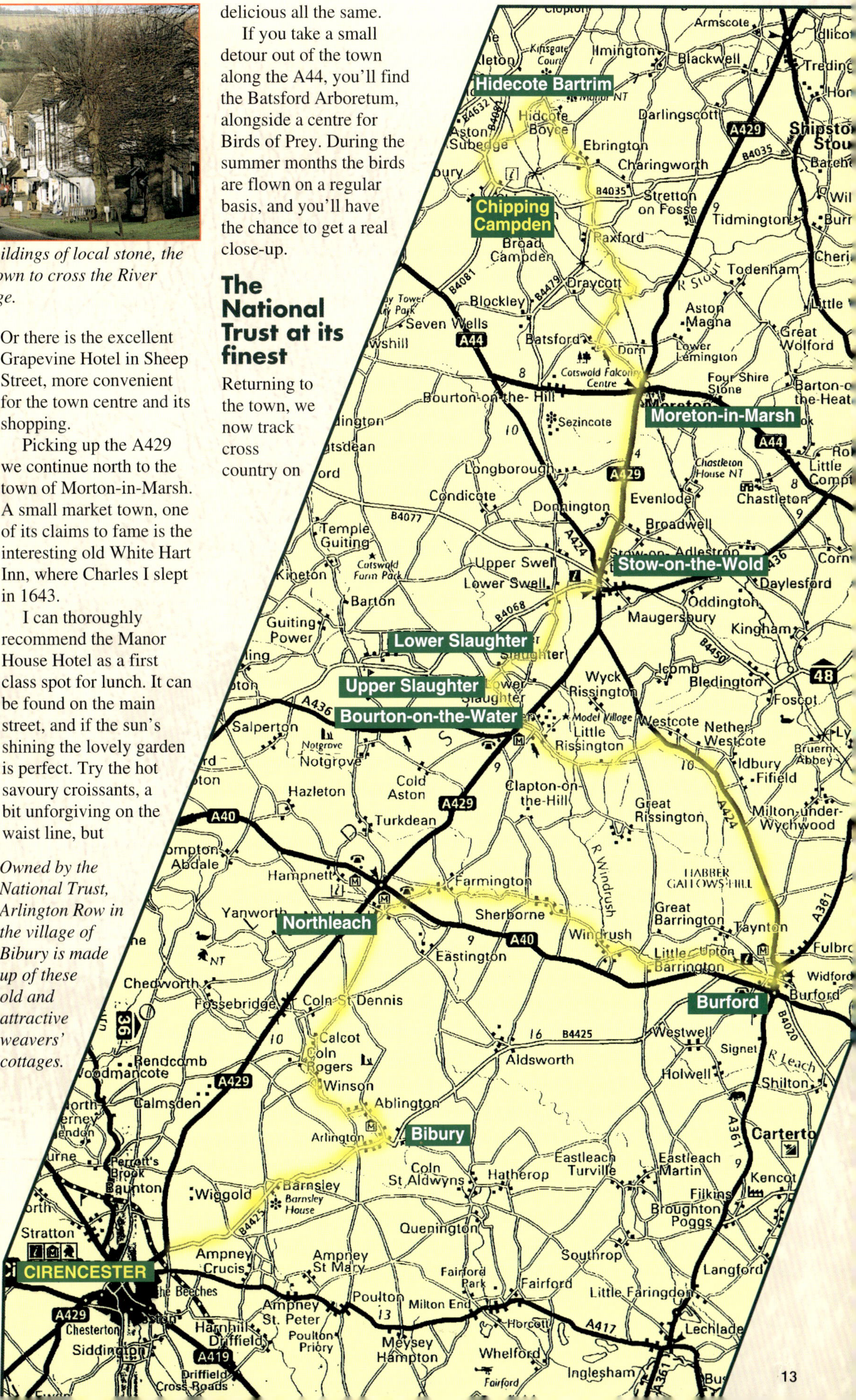

13

Enjoying your Jaguar
continued

In the village of Bibury, the Swan Hotel stands on the edge of the River Coln.

There are seemingly miles of hedges in the outstanding gardens of Hidcote Manor. The sound-deadening qualities of the hedges add to the tranquillity of this beautiful place. It must take a small army to keep them trimmed.

picturesque narrow lanes via Draycot, Paxford and Ebrington, to Hidcote Bartrim for the last leg of today's journey. Here you will find the late-17th century Hidcote Manor. Now owned by the National Trust, the formal gardens are stunning and well worth a visit.

We round off the day by taking a short drive into the beautiful town of Chipping Campden.

Once again it was wool that made Chipping Campden wealthy. History abounds here, typified by the 14th century Woolstaplers Hall and the 15th century wool church, whose imposing steeple can be seen for many miles around. Close to the church can be found what is left of Campden House, burned down in 1645 by its owner, rather than see it fall into Parliamentarian hands.

In the centre of the main street, close to the arched market hall, you will find the three-red-star Cotswold House Hotel, ideal for an overnight stop, or as a base for exploring the surrounding area.

My wife and I were fortunate enough to choose it for a two-night stay with 20 friends, in order to celebrate our recent 25th wedding anniversary. Each attractive bedroom has its own theme, the public rooms are exquisite and there are beautiful arrangements of fresh flowers everywhere. And with food and service to match, I cannot recommend this hotel highly enough.

Perhaps the area is a bit spoilt for choice when it comes to fine hotels. A short car ride from Chipping Campden, sitting on top of Willersey Hill, you could always try the Dormy House Hotel, a converted 17th century farm house, its 'Tapestries' restaurant has an enviable reputation, and rightly so in my opinion.

Well that's our second journey finished, and I do hope you will want to try it for yourselves sometime.

For our next feature, we travel to the South East of England to look at a county that I often ignore, mainly because I live there. Yet Kent is without doubt a very attractive area and worth closer scrutiny. Join me soon for a look at the 'Chocolate Box' villages of the Garden of England and its historic coastline. ●

The 15th Century Wool Church at Chipping Campden.

From Cirencester to Chipping Campden

Hotels *(SP = secure parking)*

Swan Hotel 01285 740695	Bibury	Two-star
Bibury Court 01285 740337	Bibury	Two-star / *SP*
Wyck Hill House 01451 831936	Stow-on-the-Wold	Four-star / *SP*
Grapevine Hotel 01451 830344	Stow-on-the-Wold	Three-star
Manor House Hotel 01608 650501	Morton-in-Marsh	Three-star
Cotswold House Hotel 01386 840330	Chipping Campden	Three-red-star / *SP*
Dormy House Hotel 01386 852711	Willersey Hill	Three-star / *SP*

Places of interest

Corinium Museum — Cirencester
Open April-Oct, Mon-Sat 10am-5pm, Sun 2-5pm.

Arlington Row — Bibury
Just walk up the village street.

Arlington Mill — Bibury

Museum of Mechanical Music — Northleach
Open every day except Christmas, 10am-6pm.

Cotswold Motor Museum — Bourton-on-the-Water
Open March-Nov 10am-5pm, Dec-Feb weekends only.

Batsford Arboretum — Morton-in-Marsh
Open March to early Nov daily, 10am-5pm.

Hidcote Manor — Hidcote Bartrim
Open April-end Oct daily, except Tues and Fri, 11am-7pm.

Woolstaplers Hall — Chipping Campden
Open April-Oct daily 11am-6pm.

The villages
Cirencester, Bibury, Northleach, Burford, Bourton-on-the-Water, Lower and Upper Slaughter, Stow-on-the-Wold, Morton-in-Marsh, Hidcote Bartrim, Chipping Campden.

Kelsey Classic Car Storage

Kelsey Classic Car Storage is now taking bookings for storage in its brand-new purpose-built car storage facility.

Providing the finest car storage in the UK, it is located in a quiet setting that is only 15 miles from central London and just 10 minutes from the M25 motorway network. Access to the major international airports could not be easier, and the busy Biggin Hill airport is less than five minutes away.

Safeguarding the cars in our care has been a major consideration during the planning. With the owners living on-site and the use of the latest high tech security systems, 24-hour cover is provided, making this the very best environment for the storage, protection and maintenance of classic and cherished cars.

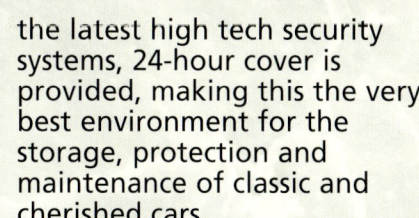

Features include a rolling road, full de-humidifying system and private exercise road.

In addition to basic car storage from £19.50 per week, a wide range of other services are available, from simple valeting to a full car care and maintenance programme, MoT testing and a delivery and collection service for both cars and drivers.

Administered by classic car owners with a sympathy for the care and well-being of fine cars, it is truly a facility run by enthusiasts for enthusiasts.

www.kelsey.co.uk/storage *or for a brochure with further details contact:*

Kelsey Classic Car Storage

Tel: **01959 541444**. **Fax:** **01959 541400** (International calls: 0044 1959 541444)
or e-mail: **storage@kelsey.co.uk**

Enjoying your Jaguar

Jerry Stamper takes you on a short tour recommended to help you get the most pleasure and enjoyment out of your Jaguar.

Part Three:
Kent, the Garden of England.

The wonderful village square of Chilham, full of Tudor character and with a Jacobean mansion on its eastern edge

Early Spring with oast houses in a typical Kent Landscape.

I am sure that I am no different to anyone else when looking at the county you live in. Being so familiar with Kent, its towns and villages, I suppose it's the old saying that 'familiarity breeds contempt'. Contempt is too strong a word for it, but certainly an element of 'taking it for granted' creeps in all too easily over the years and many treasures can get overlooked.

As to people living outside the county, I've no doubt that Kent consists of little more than the A2/M2 or M20, en-route to the channel ports and, like a laxative, is passed through as quickly as possible.

A tour of discovery

However, when I sat back and took proper stock of the county, I realised just how fortunate I am to live in such a beautiful part of England. So I set off in my XJ40 for this, our third outing in the series. I hope to share with you some of the attractions I explored.

For outing number three, we'll start the journey from Dover, travelling through Canterbury and the Weald of Kent to one of the county's most famous and historic castles.

Throughout the area most of the best places to stay are B&Bs, and believe me there are many which are nothing short of superb.

However, if you want a hotel that's a bit special, I would recommend Chilston Park near Maidstone. A quite magnificent Grade 1 listed mansion, it was built in the 13th century and remodelled in the 18th. Full of many interesting *objets d'art*. At

dusk each day over 200 candles are lit, giving the whole hotel a unique ambience.

A very historic port

At first glance the town of Dover itself may appear to have very little to recommend it, being no more than one of the country's busiest seaports. However, being where it is, its history is boundless.

Evidence of occupation by the Romans, Saxons and Normans is everywhere. Dover's most famous feature is, of course, Dover Castle, perched on the cliffs high above the Eastern Docks. It was the Normans who constructed the keep at the centre of the Castle in 1168. From then it was in continuous military use until 1958, an unbroken history of some 790 years.

Well worth a visit, the castle features 'Hellfire Corner', a network of tunnels constructed during the Napoleonic era and used for various purposes including the headquarters of the Dunkirk evacuation, during WW2.

The Five Ports

From Dover we take the A258 north, to pass through Walmer and Deal with their small Tudor forts and on to Sandwich. Along with Dover, Hythe, New Romney and Hastings, Sandwich forms part of the medieval defensive confederation known as the 'Cinque' or five Ports.

Sandwich itself is now some one mile inland, due to the silting of the River Stour, on which the town stands. However, it is a most attractive little market town, and there is the famous Royal St George golf course close by.

Walmer castle became the official residence of the Lord Warden of the Cinque Ports in 1730. And today the honorary title of Lord Warden is held by HRH Queen Elizabeth The Queen Mother and was once held by Sir Winston Churchill.

From Sandwich take the A257 to Canterbury, passing through Wingham en-route. Here you will find the *Red Lion*; good beer and food are served in this characterful 15th century pub.

A Canterbury tale

Canterbury itself should be on everyone's list of places to visit. Surrounding its cathedral, seat of the Primate of all England, are narrow lanes crammed with medieval and Tudor architecture.

Other attractions include the Canterbury Tales Exhibition,

17

Enjoying your Jaguar
continued

The M20 brings us into Dover, with its castle perched above the busy town.

The Village Sign. The maids of Biddenden were Siamese twins born in 1135. Joined at the hip and shoulder, they survived until the age of 34. Income from land they bequeathed provided bread and cheese for the poor of the parish.

On the outskirts of Smarden. This is just one of the many 'chocolate box' cottages in the area.

Weavers' cottages in the main street of Biddenden. Many have been converted into restaurants and shops.

where the sights, sounds and smells of 17th century Canterbury are vividly brought to life.

Accommodation in the town is mostly B&Bs and small hotels, or you might like to try Howfield Manor just a couple of miles outside the town in the village of Chartham Hatch. Originally part of a priory, its history dates back some 800 years.

Where pilgrims trod

Leaving Canterbury south on the A28, keep an eye open for the right hand turn onto the A252. Shortly after joining the A252 look out for the sign posts to Chilham.

Situated a short distance off the main road, Chilham is on the old 'Pilgrims Way' and is a gem. Its square of half-timbered houses date from late-medieval times. In one corner of the square next to the 15th century church you'll find the *White Horse* where they serve fine pub lunches. Opposite is the entrance to Chilham Castle, a red brick Jacobean mansion, built in 1616.

The mansion contains the Kent Battle of Britain Museum, and in the grounds there is a collection of Birds of Prey. On several days throughout the year there are also displays of medieval jousting.

Rejoin the A252 and drive south through Challock Lees until you reach the A20 at Charing. Turn left on to the A20, then a couple of hundred yards on take the right hand turn sign-posted Pluckley.

In the footsteps of 'Pop' Larkin

Arriving in Pluckley there is a turning on the left, where you will find the *Black Horse* pub, another good stop for lunch. Around the walls you will see a number of pictures taken during the filming of the famous *The Darling Buds of May* television series. It was a farm in Pluckley where the series was based and the *Black Horse* was a regular haunt for the cast.

On the outskirts of the village, and well sign posted, is a great B&B. Elvey Farm Country Hotel is situated on a working farm, with the accommodation located in an Oast House, converted stables and an old Kent barn. Evening meals are available on request and, like the breakfasts, are served in the unique dining room.

Keep on the main road and find your way to Smarden. On the way you will pass any number of the most beautiful 'chocolate box' cottages, roses round the door - all looking idyllic.

The village itself was once a market town. Licensed by Edward II in 1332, it was particularly noted for its cloth trade. Standing to the west of the churchyard you will find one of the finest surviving examples of a cloth hall, with the cloth hoist still hanging from its gable end. The pathway from the Cloth Hall to the 14th century St Michael's church is paved with local limestone containing fossilised snails.

Continuing through the village stay on the main road until you meet the A274. Turn left into Biddenden.

A land of bread and cheese

Biddenden is another fascinating village built on the medieval cloth trade. Many of the timber framed buildings date from the 15th century. The sign on the village green depicts the famous Biddenden Maids. Born about 1135, Mary and Elizabeth Chulkhurst were Siamese twins, joined at the hip and shoulder, they

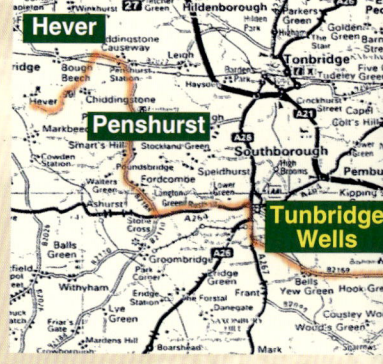

An imposing entrance to the precinct of Canterbury Cathedral. Unusually these days, you will have to pay to see more, and to take photographs of the interior.

survived until the age of 34 and died within a few hours of each other. They bequeathed a number of acres known as the Bread and Cheese Land, income from which provided bread and cheese for the poor of the parish.

We leave Biddenden west on the A262 heading in the direction of Lamberhurst. Just a few miles along the road you will find Sissinghurst Castle, the home since the 1920s of Vita Sackville-West who, with her husband, turned the rather neglected gardens into one of Englands finest. Needless to say, the gardens can get very busy during the months of July and August.

Continuing on the A262 until you reach the A21, here you turn left and follow the road into Lamberhurst. Situated a little way south of the village on the A21, Scotney Castle can be found. The ruined 14th century tower and attached 17th century house, are surrounded by a moat and landscaped garden. The trees and flowering shrubs make an attractive backdrop, and Scotney has long been a favourite with artists.

Kent's Royal Spa

From Scotney Castle, pick up the B2169 west in the direction of Tunbridge Wells. At the junction with the A267 turn right and make your way into the town.

Royal Tunbridge Wells has been a fashionable spa town since the 17th century, when it became popular with royalty and the aristocracy. Amongst the many interesting places to visit there is The Pantiles, the town's famous colonnaded shopping street, where you can still 'take the waters'. Naturally there are many attractive places for lunch.

For an overnight stay there is the Spa Hotel, originally built as a country mansion in 1766 and still retaining much of its Georgian and Regency character. It has a heated indoor swimming pool, sauna, solarium and gym for the use of guests.

Leaving Tunbridge Wells on the A264, turn right at Langton Green,

The Black Horse at Pluckley. Note the unusual shape of the windows, which are found throughout the village. Known as 'lucky' windows, it is through one such window that a member of a local family escaped from Parliamentarians during the Civil war.

Another view of the village of Chilham.

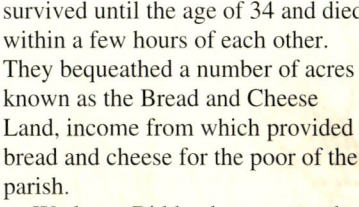

A detail from one of the beautiful stained glass windows to be found in Canterbury Cathedral.

19

Enjoying your Jaguar
continued

Set in acres of parkland, Chilston Park is a Grade 1 classic 17th century country house hotel which is lit by hundreds of candles each night.

Kent

Hotels *(SP = secure parking)*
Chilston Park *s/p*	Lenham	01622 858588
Howfield Manor *s/p*	Canterbury	01227 738294
Elvey Farm Country Hotel *s/p*	Pluckley	01233 840442
Spa Hotel	Tunbridge Wells	01892 520331

The best B&Bs
Tram Hatch	Charing Heath	01233 713373
Hancocks Farmhouse	Cranbrook	01580 714645
Swale Cottage	Penshurst	01892 870738
Jordans	Plaxtol	01732 810379

The villages
Walmer, Deal, Sandwich, Chilham, Pluckley, Smarden, Biddenden, Lamberhurst, Fordcombe, Penshurst, Chiddingstone, Hever.

Places of interest
Dover Castle	Easter-Sept. Daily. 10am-6pm
	Oct-Easter. Daily. 10am-4pm
Walmer Castle	Easter-Sept. Daily. 10am-6pm
	Oct-Easter. Tue-Sun. 10am-4pm
Deal Castle	Easter-Sept. Daily. 10am-6pm
	Oct-Easter. Tue-Sun. 10am-4pm
Canterbury Tale' Exhibition	Apr-Sept. Daily. 9.30am-6.30pm
	Oct-Mar. Daily. 10am-4.30pm
Chilham Castle	Apr-Oct. Daily. 11am-6pm, Grounds and Museum
Sissinghurst Gardens	Apr-Oct. Tue-Fri. 1pm-6.30pm, Sat-Sun. 10am-5.30pm
Scotney Castle	Apr-Nov. Wed-Fri. 11am-6pm, Sat-Sun. 2pm-6pm
The Pantiles	
Penshurst Place	Apr-Oct. Daily. 1pm - 5.30pm (House)
	Apr-Oct. Daily. 11am - 6pm (Grounds)
Chiddingstone Castle	
Hever Castle	Mar-Nov. Daily. Noon-6.30pm

heading north on the B2188. Passing through Fordcombe and Smarts Hill, you will eventually reach the village of Penshurst. Here it will be hard to miss Penshurst Place. Built in the 14th century, it has been the home of the Sidney family for more than 400 years. The magnificent Tudor gardens are one of the oldest in private ownership in Britain. Also to be found in the village are numerous tea shops, and the 12th century village church.

Nagging wives take heed

We now follow the B2176 north to Chiddingstone Causeway, here we turn left on the B2027, and shortly after turn left again, driving into the village of Chiddingstone.

This National Trust village has a beautifully preserved main street, with buildings dating from the 16th and 17th century. At the end of the street you will find the *Castle Inn*, a wonderful old pub for either lunch or an evening meal. A pint of well-kept Harveys Sussex beer slides down too easily at any time of the day. Access to the 19th century Chiddingstone Castle is a short drive further on. Interestingly, behind the street can be found a large sandstone rock, known as the Chiding Stone, it is where the village got its name. And it was here that nagging wives were once brought to be 'chided' by the entire population of the village.

The haunt of XKs

For the last leg of this mini tour we drive north to Bough Beech, then follow the sign-posts to Hever.

Yet another fine pub, the *Henry VIII*, stands on a corner opposite the village church. However, just one hundred yards further on is the entrance to Hever Castle. Chosen by *Jaguar Monthly* for the start in June 1998 of the XK-50th Anniversary Taste of England tour, the castle and its gardens are stunning.

This moated 13th century Tudor castle was the childhood home of Anne Boleyn, second wife of Henry VIII, and mother of Queen Elizabeth I.

The castle deteriorated over the years, along with the fortunes of the Boleyn family. It wasn't until the early part of this century that William Waldorf Astor, a wealthy American, bought and restored the building and its extensive grounds. The Italian Garden, Lake and Maze are all wonderful attractions in themselves.

The castle contains many memories of Anne Boleyn, including portraits and the 'Book of Hours' taken by her to her execution.

Perhaps a sad note to close on, but that concludes our third jaunt. Next time we will be making our way north, to spend some time in the breathtaking Yorkshire Moors. ●

Penshurst, situated on the North Weald. G646 is parked outside the village Post Office, the building dating from the early 1800. In the background, the entrance to Penshurst Place, ancestral home of the Sidney family for more than 400 years.

The entrance to Hever Castle (closed until the beginning of April). Here you can visit the home of Anne Boleyn, second wife of Henry VIII.

The exquisite village of Smarden. Once famous for it's cloth trade, it is now a sleepy little Kentish hamlet, though full of the most stunning architecture.

The grounds of Hever Castle. This was the start point of the XK-50th Anniversary Taste of England tour during 1998. The Tudor castle makes a perfect backdrop for the XKs.

Enjoying your Jag

Jerry Stamper's intimate knowledge of the
dates back to his days in the Cava
many civilian tours there in mo
so it was a natural choice for ar
for Jaguar M

The York

An old flax mill in Nidderdale, just north of Patley Bridge. It is now converted to a pub, where good honest Yorkshire food is on offer.

I was first introduced to Yorkshire and its breathtaking scenery at a time when I appreciated it far less than I do now.

If you're old enough to remember the winter of 1961/62, it was perhaps one of the worst for many years. Several feet of snow covered northern England and I had to endure the dubious pleasure of spending six months at the second home of the British Army, Catterick Garrison.

A 27-litre V12 Rolls Royce Meteor engine, along with a Morris Eight unit just to charge the batteries, powered my transport in those days. I speak of course of a 50-ton Centurion tank, the ultimate off-roader. Fine for cross-country driving, but unspeakably cold during those dreadful winter months.

Since those days long past it has been my good fortune, on a number of occasions, to enjoy the stunning scenery this most attractive part of the British Isles has to offer.

So join me once again for a closer look. But don't forget to fill the petrol tank before setting off.

Take my breath away (to steal a phrase)

We'll start the tour from the spa town of Harrogate, driving through the unique splendour of the Yorkshire Dales National Park. Using mainly 'B' roads and unclassified roads, we'll be visiting Wharfedale and Nidderdale. In contrast to the three previous tours, there are fewer places of interest to visit, this time the emphasis being on quite unbelievable scenery.

The Floral Resort of England

Nowadays Harrogate is famous mainly as a conference centre, yet its history stretches back to the 16th century when its mineral springs were discovered. The growth of the

One of the many bridges spanning the River Cover in Coverdale, magnificent driving country in summer and winter.

town's prosperity has resulted in a wealth of attractive stone buildings, along with many beautiful gardens. And the country's first public baths were built here in 1842.

Needless to say, there are many excellent hotels, perhaps the most famous being the four-star *Old Swan Hotel*, where Agatha Christie once stayed. Situated in the centre of the town, it is noted for its elegance and good standard of cuisine.

We leave the town on the A61 travelling south to join the A658. In the village of Pool turn right on the A659 to Otley. This old market town is now largely swamped by modern industry, but has a very interesting church. The churchyard contains a rather odd memorial to the men who, between 1845 and 1849, died while digging the Bramhope railway tunnel.

Tranquillity in Lower Wharfdale

Taking the B6451 north, we soon turn left on the unclassified road through Weston, Askwith, Middleton, Langbar and Beamsley. It's a narrow road and will require some care when driving, but the views of the river Wharf on the left really are wonderful. On reaching the A59 turn left to the roundabout. Here we turn north on the B6160.

Still in the Wharf valley we reach Bolton Abbey. Much of this 12th century Augustinian priory now lies in ruins, but for hundreds of years the Nave has served as a parish church. Standing by a bend in the river it provides the most tranquil of settings.

Also to be found near the Abbey is the *Devonshire Arms*, a three-red-star hotel owned by the Duke and Duchess of Devonshire. It stands in 12 acres of parkland, and antiques and paintings from Chatsworth in the public rooms and bedrooms add to the country house atmosphere.

To the heart of The National Park

Continuing on the B6160 to Bardon Tower, a ruined 15th century hunting lodge. Turn left on the unclassified road to Eastby and on to Stirton. Here we turn right and join the B6265. At Rylstone turn left to Hetton, where the *Angle* pub

23

Enjoying your Jaguar
continued

The village of Malham, with G464 parked outside the now-derelict smithy.

High in Nidderdale on the road from Patley Bridge to Lofthouse – not another car in sight.

is to be found – it serves wonderful food and more than 20 different wines by the glass. From Hetton turn right to Winterburn, following the road to Airton, Kirkby Malham and Malham.

You may want to leave your car in the large car park alongside the National Park Centre and have a stroll around this attractive village, which stands among some of the most rugged scenery in Yorkshire.

On the northern edge of the village you'll find the Malham Centre, a huge clothing shop which also contains its own tea-shop. Just the spot for morning coffee or, if the wind is chilly, how about a mug of hot chocolate? Great to get cold hands around.

There are also two cosy inns in the village, one dating from 1723. The other, the *Buck Inn*, is popular with walkers. In the lounge bar they serve no less than 78 varieties of single malt whisky… at least, that's how many I counted.

Over the top

Staying on the main road, we leave Malham, heading north on the unclassified road sign-posted Malham Tarn. Immediately, the road starts to climb, twisting and turning towards the tarn, a natural lake lying high on the fells. Follow the sign-posts in the direction of Arncliffe.

The higher we climb the bleaker the scenery becomes. However, the never-ending dry stone walls break the rather featureless landscape. I can't help thinking that keeping them in good repair must be a little like painting the Forth Bridge.

From time to time we come across small farms, isolated in the extreme. At one point it looks as if the road is closed, and you'll have to get out of the car to open the gate that bars your way. Not forgetting to close it behind you, we continue ever higher.

From the top of the pass the views are simply stunning. We now start to descend towards Arncliff on fairly precarious narrow roads. However, they present no problem if you drive sensibly.

Forward to the past

Arncliff is perhaps one of the most idyllic villages in the Dales. Driving through, if it wasn't for the cars, you would think time had stood still. As you enter the village, the first house on the left is an unobtrusive little tea room, providing excellent snack lunches and afternoon teas. There is also a good pub in the village. So park the car and enjoy a walk round this historic little hamlet.

Continuing through the village, drive straight on along the Skirfare valley until you reach the B6160 just north of Kilnsey. Here we turn left and make our way to Kettlewell, another outstanding Dale's village.

Like Arncliff it too seems to have been passed by time. It first came to prominence in the 17th century as a market town and centre for lead mining. Once again it's worth parking the car for a walk round. Although a small village, it boasts no

Sparkling streams abound. Another view of Coverdale.

less than three inns. In addition there is the Langcliffe Country Hotel, an AA-selected b&b; the rooms have splendid views across the surrounding fells.

Although not on our route today, a narrow road runs north from Kettlewell quickly climbing to over

The Wolverine Cave in Stump Cross caverns. You'll find it on the road between Grassington and Ripon.

Voted 'The most beautiful village in Britain' in 1949, Linton near Grassington has changed little since then.

1,600 feet before it descends steeply into Wensleydale.

However, we will be turning south on the unclassified road, which runs parallel to the B6160, with the river Wharf on your right. As we drive towards Conistone, on the other side of the river, one of the most striking features that you can't help but see is Kilnsey Crag. A huge rock outcrop, it is among the most dramatic rock formations in the country.

Continuing along the road we make our way to Grassington.

Any old iron

This popular tourist centre has been settled since early times, with much evidence of iron-age settlements to be found. One of the largest villages in the Dales, there are plenty of shops, teashops, pubs and hotels to be found. Perhaps it is not the most beautiful on the outskirts, but the village has a most attractive Georgian centre, with its cobbled market square. Definitely a place to visit, it has a lively, bustling atmosphere.

Situated just a short distance from Grassington is the tiny hamlet of Linton-In-Craven. Voted the 'Loveliest Village in the North' way back in 1949, it's the same today as it was then.

In the centre of the village there's an unusually large almshouse, endowed by Richard Fountaine in 1721. Local legend has it that Fountaine's fame and fortune was made burying plague victims in London. Yet nearer to the truth is the fact that arriving in London he became a timber merchant, making his money selling timber for both coffins during the plague, and for house building following the Great Fire of 1666.

His name is remembered now in the name of the village inn *The Fountaine*. A very popular pub, it has

Looking down on the tiny hamlet of Arncliffe, situated on the River Skirfare in Littondale.

The bustling market town of Grassington, with its cobbled square. There's plenty of parking in the car park on the outskirts of the town, and a number of pubs and restaurants for a lunch stop.

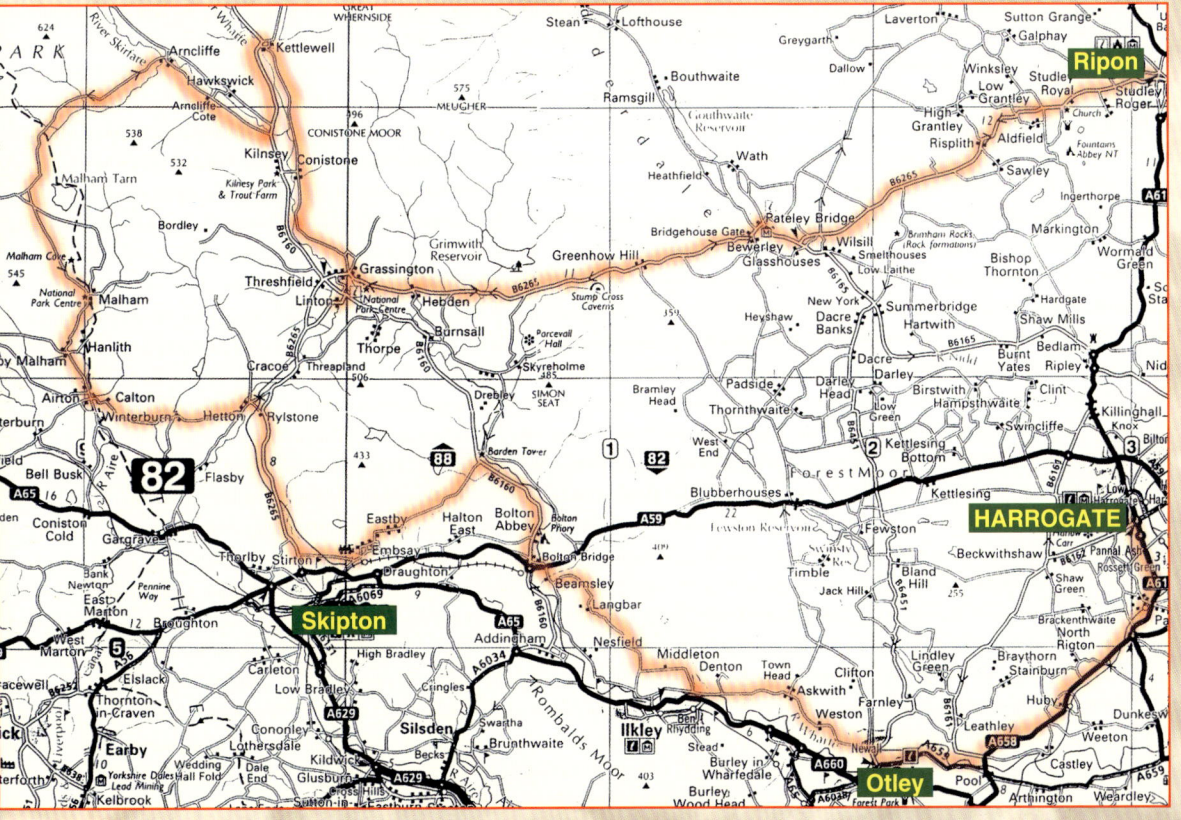

25

Enjoying your Jaguar
continued

Arncliffe is a village that time has passed by.

an extremely warm and friendly atmosphere, while the food and beer are also of a very high standard.

Rock with a caveman

From Grassington we pick up the B6265 east towards Pateley Bridge. *En route* will be found Stumps Cross Caverns. Although the caverns extend some three miles into the hillside, only one quarter-mile section of the dramatic stalactite and stalagmite filled caverns is open to the public. Nonetheless, it's one of the country's most interesting show caves.

Continuing on the B6252 we find our way to Pateley Bridge, a pleasant old market town, and centre of Nidderdale everyday life. You could always visit the Nidderdale museum, where over 3,000 items relating to Yorkshire Dale's life are on display.

We'll round off tour number four by taking the B6265 to the town of Ripon, visiting Fountains Abbey on the way.

This 12th-to-15th century Cistercian abbey is reckoned to be the finest in England. It graphically demonstrates Norman and medieval monastic life. It's a real must on anyone's list of places to visit. Adjacent to the abbey is Studley Royal, a magnificent garden, landscaped in the 18th century. Following the dissolution of the monasteries in the 17th century, stones from the abbey were used to build the nearby Fountains Hall.

We conclude our journey in Ripon, popularly known as the gateway to the Dales.

There is plenty to see and do in this attractive city. From its 12th century cathedral with a Saxon crypt, reckoned to be the earliest Christian architecture in the country, to the Prison and Police museum, that can be found housed in the old prison building, dating from 1686.

The Ripon Spa Hotel, situated just five minutes walk from the town centre, is the largest in the area. It still maintains some of its original Edwardian splendour, although perhaps now a little faded. However, the service is friendly and efficient, and the food extremely good with very generous portions.

This particular outing has only scratched the surface of this most gorgeous part of the country. So for our next day out we'll stay in the Dales and travel further north, to look at Wensleydale and Coverdale. ●

Yorkshire Dales

Hotels

The Old Swan	Harrogate	01423 500055
Devonshire Arms	Bolton Abbey	01756 710441
Langcliff Country Hotel	Kettlewell	01756 760243
Ripon Spa Hotel	Ripon	01765 602172

The villages
Otley, Bolton Abbey, Hetton, Malham, Arncliff, Kettlewell, Conistone, Grassington, Linton, Pateley Bridge.

Places of interest

Bolton Abbey	Open all year round.
Bardon Tower	Open all year round.
National Parks Centre, Malham	Open all year round.
Malham Cove	
Stumps Cross Caverns	April-October, daily. November-March, Sat & Sun.
Nidderdale Museum, Patley Bridge	Easter to September, 2-5pm.
Fountains Abbey	Open daily from 10am.
Studley Royal	Open daily from 10am.
Prison & Police Museum, Ripon	May-September, Tue-Sun pm.
Ripon Cathedral	All year round.

The popular walking centre of Malham sits amongst some of the most rugged scenery to be found anywhere in England.

With views like this you could sit all day, the scenery seems to change with the light, minute by minute. Looking down on Scar House Reservoir in Nidderdale

How can you pay less for a copy of JAGUAR WORLD MONTHLY?

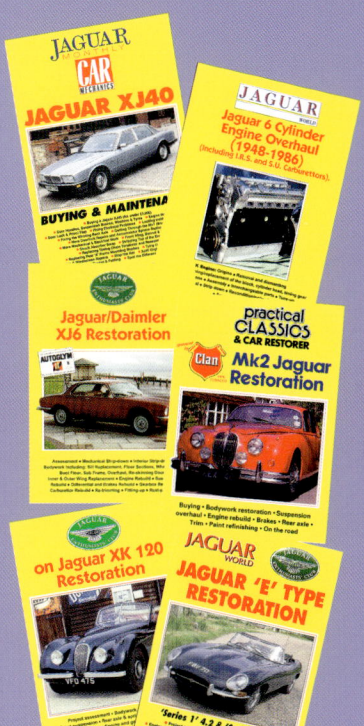

Choose 14 issues for the price of 12 and save around 30%*, OR opt for a FREE Jaguar book and save 20%* an issue – you save either way!

Jaguar World Monthly is the complete guide to Jaguar of all ages:

- News on the latest models
- Comparison road tests
- Informative buying guides
- Essential tips on maintenance
- Free technical helpline service
- Regular restoration features

All this and much more!

☎ **Call our subscriptions hotline today!**
+ 44 (0)1959 541444

Fax: + 44 (0) 1959 541400   e-mail: jwm.mag@kelsey.co.uk
Post coupon to: *JWM* Subscriptions, Kelsey Publishing Group, PO Box 13, Westerham, Kent TN16 3WT UK.

* Saving based on UK newsstand prices.

For up to date subscription offer details visit our website: www.kelsey.co.uk

---

Please start my *Jaguar World Monthly* subscription from the .... 2002 issue. Tick an offer below.

■ OFFER 1
Please send me 2 FREE ISSUES added to the end of my subscription

■ OFFER 2
Please send me A FREE BOOK as marked below

☐ E-Type Restoration (r.r.p £17.95)
☐ Jaguar XJ40 (r.r.p £17.95)
☐ Jaguar 6-Cylinder Engine Overhaul 1948-1986 (r.r.p £14.95)
☐ Jaguar/Daimler XJ6 Restoration (r.r.p £16.95)
☐ Mk2 Jaguar Restoration (r.r.p £16.95)
☐ Jaguar XK 120 Restoration (r.r.p £18.95)

For up to date listings of available books visit our website:
<www.kelsey.co.uk/books/index.html>

I enclose my cheque for (see rates above) £ ....
(payable to Kelsey Publishing Ltd.)

(Or) I wish to pay by credit card ☐   ☐ ☐ ☐

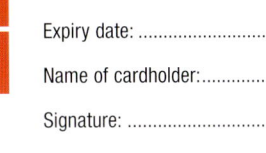

SUBSCRIPTION ORDER FORM

Card No:..
Expiry date: ....Switch issue no: ....
Name of cardholder:...
Signature: ....
Name: ....
Address:...
....
....Post code*........................
(*incorrect, incomplete or illegible post codes may result in delays in the delivery of your magazine)
Daytime Tel:.. JWM

Prices correct at time of going to press – March 2002

Enjoying your Jaguar

Our first mini tour of the Yorkshire Dales took us through Wharfedale and Nidderdale, an area made famous in more recent times by the TV soap *Emmerdale*.

For this, our second look at the 'Dales', we move further north travelling to Swaledale and Wensleydale, scene of another TV favourite of a few years ago, *All Creatures Great and Small*.

Once again it's the marvellous scenery that will feature in this particular outing. We'll start from Richmond, perhaps the most historic town in the dales. From there we'll use

Tan Hill Inn, the highest in the country and remote in the extreme. It was once used by miners who supplied coal to the local lead mining industry.

This month, Jerry Stamper takes us through Swaledale and Wensleydale.

Part Five:
The North Yorkshire Dales.

ainly 'B' roads to visit some exquisite villages and hamlets all set in quite breathtaking countryside.

Shades of the past
Writing this series of articles has made me realise just how fortunate I have been, especially during my early years. Having spent my late teens and early 20s serving in the British Army, I was privileged to live and work in parts of the UK I may never have otherwise seen. However, it's only in later years that I have really started to appreciate those times long past.

Sweet lass
For me, back in the early '60s, the town of Richmond meant little more than a bus ride from the garrison town of Catterick, to spent a not *too* sober night at the NAAFI Club on the town's outskirts.

Yet Richmond is steeped in history dating back to the 11th century and beyond.

So fascinating is this dales town that you could quite easily spend a couple of days taking in all it has to offer. Top of the list must be the extraordinary and imposing castle. The massive keep and castle walls clinging precariously to the hillside above the river Swale. Alan Rufus, the first Norman Earl of Richmond, began the building about 1070 and many of its original features remain to this day.

Much of medieval Richmond grew around the castle and from the town-square radiate narrow cobbled streets, or wynds. Other places of interest include the Georgian Theatre Royal built in 1788, the Green Howard's regimental museum and, for those of you who remember the famous old song *Sweet lass of Richmond Hill*, there's the chance to visit that original lassie's home.

For accommodation, there are a couple of hotels in the town, both two-star with the King's Head in the market square being the larger. The Frenchgate is perhaps cosier and away from the centre of the bustling town.

Alternatively, three miles outside of the town there's the Washton Springs, an AA Premier Selected B&B.

Into Herriot country
We leave Richmond, west on the A6108. Just before Downholme, turn right on to the B6270. Drive through Fremington and continue onto Reeth, a very attractive village perched on a hillside above the river Swale. At this point we fork right taking the unclassified road to Langthwaite.

It's here we enter Arkengarthdale, one of the most remote of the Yorkshire dales. Remnants of lost lead mining villages are a feature of the area. Whaw and Arkle Town are just two. Needless to say, my favourite has to be Booze, just north of Langthwaite. Now in real 'Herriot' country, the road from Langthwaite south to Low Row featured in the opening shots of *All Creatures Great and Small*.

We continue through Arkengarthdale, climbing all the time. The lonely cottages high on the slopes of the dale start to peter out and the scenery becomes bleaker. Finally we reach Tan Hill, windswept and devoid of trees – nothing seems to survive except the heather.

Yet standing out like a sore thumb there's the Tan Hill Inn. Completely

Enjoying your Jaguar
continued

The attractive village of Coniston, on the road between Grassington and Aysgarth.

Aysgarth Lower Falls. Just one in a series of three of the most beautiful waterfalls on the River Ure. In spate it becomes a raging torrent.

isolated, it stands some 1,732 feet above sea level and is England's highest inn. Naturally enough, it is not the place to visit during the snowy winter months, as it can be cut off for weeks at a time. Inside the inn the oak ceiling beams are festooned with hundreds of postcards, and on colder days a huge log fire blazes away, creating a cosy if somewhat smoky atmosphere.

High cholesterol pass

At the Tan Hill Inn we turn left and travel south in the direction of Keld. The most westerly of Swaledale's villages, it was once a Viking settlement. Indeed, its name is an old Norse word meaning a well or spring. Continue on to the village of Thwaite, where we turn right to drive over the strangely named yet spectacular Buttertubs Pass.

Linking Swaledale and Wensleydale, the pass quickly rises to 1,736 feet. You'll find the Buttertubs themselves on the righthand side of the road, as you near the top. They're a series of deep limestone shafts, fenced off for the safety of both sheep and public alike. Rumour has it that they were dug by farmers, for cooling butter on route to market. However, more likely, they're due to natural erosion caused by the action of the mountain streams.

Another of the country's highest

Descending from the pass we reach a T-junction shortly after the village of Simonstone. Here we turn right in the direction of Hardraw. Half a mile further on and we come across the Green Dragon pub. Perhaps it's not the most attractive in the dales, having a rather stark interior, but the food and beer are both of a good standard.

On payment of a 20p toll, you gain access to the pub's major asset, Hardraw Force. Reached via a footpath from the rear of the pub, Hardraw Force is the highest waterfall in the country and, at certain times of the year, you're actually able to walk behind the water. During wet winter months the falls are at their most dramatic, though in summer it can be a little different, with a mere trickle coming over the top.

Leaving the Green Dragon, continue along the same road until you reach the A684, where we take a left turn and on to Hawes.

Famous for its rope-making industry, and of course Wensleydale cheese, the history of Hawes dates back to Anglo-Saxon times. Its major development took place during the 19th century with the arrival of the railways. Well worth a visit is the Dales Countryside Museum where, amongst various exhibits, you can watch the making if the area's well-know cheese.

Now, would you believe, the shortest?

From Hawes we stay on the A684 heading east, along the Ure valley where, five miles on, we drive into Bainbridge. Here can be found the remains of a Roman Fort, evidence of their presence from AD 80, when they occupied the area for some 300 years.

Nearby there's the sparkling river Bain. At just two miles long, it's said to be the shortest in England.

During the Middle Ages, the landscape looked very different to that of today. Heavily wooded, its earliest inhabitants were foresters, and it was from them that a custom has been handed down, a custom that continues to this day. For the past 700 years, each evening between the early autumn and early spring, a huge horn is sounded to guide foresters off the fells. You'll find the

Waterfalls are so much a feature of this area – this one is at West Burton, a mile or so south of Aysgarth.

The imposing Bolton Castle, still remarkably preserved after more than 600 years. Mary, Queen of Scots was imprisoned here in 1568.

A dramatic view that is typical of the North Yorkshire dales. Is it any wonder that G646 required new brake pads shortly after our return home?

horn hanging in the bar at the Rose & Crown.

Best water in the dales

We stay on the A684 for a further five miles, to reach one of the Yorkshire dales' finest and most attractive waterfalls.

As you enter the village of Aysgarth, turn left at the YHA, and follow the signs to the falls. As you drive down into the valley and across the bridge, the odd glimpse of the falls through the trees only serves to stimulate the imagination. Drive on and follow the signs to the car park. Here you'll find a most interesting Dales National Park Centre. There's a footpath back to the bridge, where on the other side a cafe and museum are to be found. The museum, housed in an old mill, has a fabulous collection of horse-drawn carriages from the mundane to the most lavish.

It's here that the river Ure sweeps through a narrow mile-long limestone gorge, and over three separate falls – the Upper, Mid and Lower, known as Aysgarth Force.

Each of the three waterfalls is accessible by footpaths adjacent to

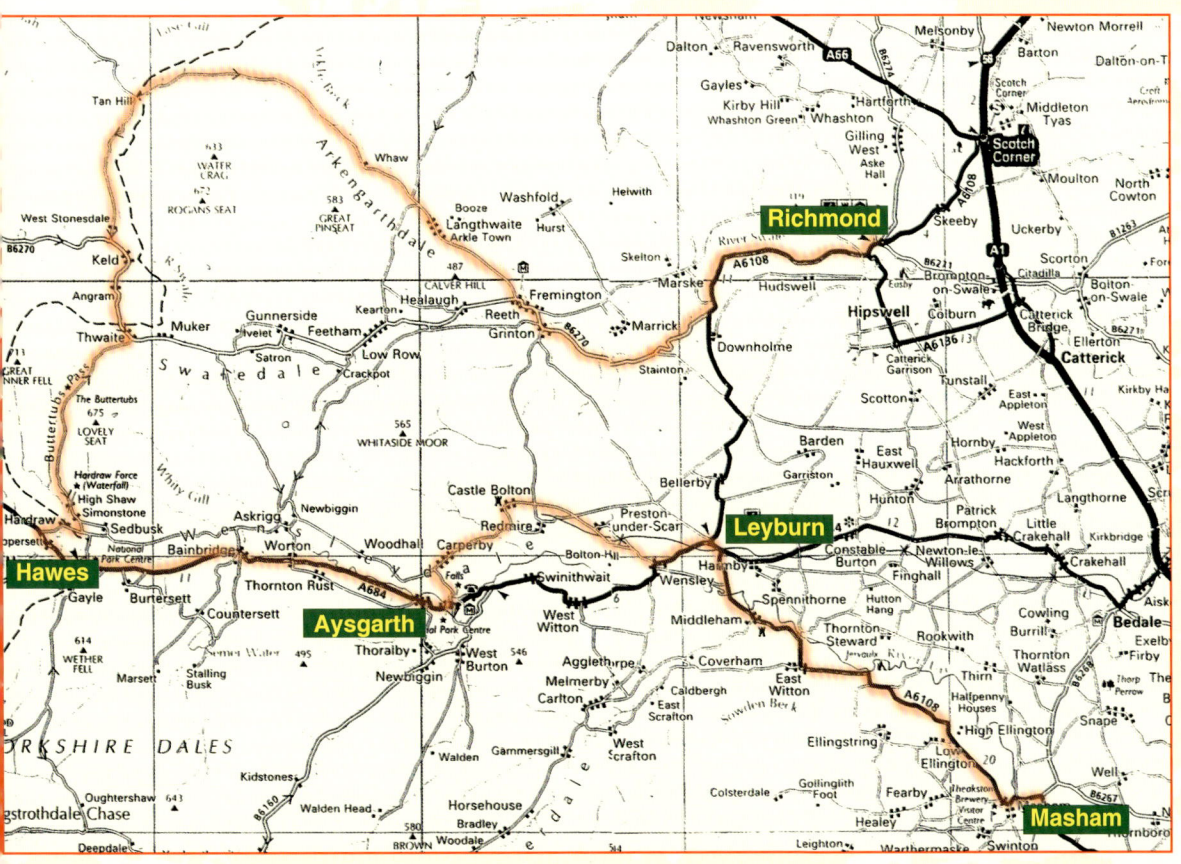

Enjoying your Jaguar
continued

Carol Stamper inside the Tan Hill Inn, with some of the hundreds of postcards hanging from the ceiling.

North Yorkshire Dales

Hotels

The King's Head	Richmond	01748 850220	Two-star.
The Frenchgate	Richmond	01748 822087	Two-star.
Washton Springs b&b	Richmond	01748 822884	Premier Selected.
Golden Lion	Leyburn	01969 22161	One-star.
King's Head	Masham	01765 689295	Two-star.

The villages
Fremington, Reeth, Langthwaite, Tan Hill, Keld, Thwaite, Hardraw, Hawes, Bainbridge, Aysgarth, Castle Bolton, Wensley, Middleham, Masham.

Places of interest

Richmond Castle, Richmond	April-Oct, daily 10am-6pm Nov-Mar, Tue-Sun 10am-4.pm.
Theatre Royal, Richmond (tours)	May-Sept, Mon-Fri 2.30pm-5pm Sat 10.30am-1.30pm.
Green Howards' Museum, Richmond	
Tan Hill Inn, Tan Hill	Normal licensing hours.
Buttertubs	Anytime.
Hardraw Force, Hardraw	Pretty much anytime.
Dales Countryside Museum, Hawes	Easter-Oct, daily 9am-5pm.
Roman Fort, Bainbridge	Anytime.
Dales National Park Centre, Aysgarth	April-Oct, daily 10am-5.30pm.
Aysgarth Falls, Aysgarth	Anytime.
Bolton Castle, castle Bolton	
Norman castle, Middleham	April-Sept, daily 10am-6pm Oct-Mar, Tue-Sun 10am-4pm.
Jervaulx Abbey, nr East Whitton	
Theakston's Brewery, Masham	By appointment.

the main car park, and believe me, it's worth leaving the car to visit perhaps the most picturesque area of north Yorkshire.

A very famous prisoner

Turning left out of the car park we take the road to Carperby and on towards Low Bolton and Redmire. Shortly before Low Bolton we turn left to make our way to Castle Bolton.

I've no doubt that if the weather's fine, you'll have spotted our next destination from some miles away. Bolton Castle is a real stunner, although in bad weather it can look rather foreboding.

England's Lord Chancellor, Richard Scrope built it in 1379, and it was here in 1568 that Mary Queen of Scots was imprisoned for six long months. The castle is extremely well preserved, and the original dinning room is now a restaurant.

The village, consisting of a single street with its cottages clustered round the green, is also particularly attractive and well worth a stroll around.

Continue through Castle Bolton travelling east, and make your way through Preston-under-Scar and on to Wensley.

Lost to the plague

Almost all of the dales get their names from the river running through them. However, Wensleydale is an exception, getting its name from the village of Wensley. Small and attractive and relatively unimportant now, during the 14th century Wensley was the market town of the dale, remaining so for some 200 years. Its decline started during the 1560s when it was blighted by the plague. The majority of its inhabitants moved to Leyburn just a couple of miles north-east, which was to become established as the new market town.

A symbol of Wensley's past glory must be its parish church. Holy Trinity dates back to the middle of the 13th century and has many notable features. These include 16th century choir stalls, rude screen and ancient box pews.

Staying on the A684 we arrive in Leyburn, which is now the principal market town and administrative centre of the dale.

The cup that cheers

Whenever I visit Leyburn, my mind goes back to the early '60s. Learning to drive three-ton lorries during a terrible winter, we would frequently stop in one of the town's cafes for a steaming hot 'cuppa'. Frozen to the marrow from sitting in the back of an open truck waiting our turn in the cab, we would warm ourselves in the cafe with liberal amounts of whisky poured into our tea. Having paid the

Looking down on Kettlewell. We stayed here overnight on our mini-tour.

Hardraw Force, the highest waterfall in the country. Very spectacular during the winter months, it is less so during the summer when barely a trickle is evident.

Bainbridge, and another superb waterfall. The village also contains the remains of a Norman castle.

The Buttertubs. Well, at least one of them. You'll find them all at the top of the spectacular pass of the same name.

bill, we would leave the empty cups stinking of scotch, and sterilised for the next customer.

Around the area are any number of attractive b&bs. Or there is the one-star Golden Lion hotel, which stands in the Market Square and dates from 1765.

The town of Leyburn itself, though busy, has a certain charm. Within easy walking distance there's a massive limestone scar known as the Shawl, from where there are quite exceptional views of Wensleydale. Local legend has it that 'The Shawl' derives its name from a shawl lost by Mary Queen of Scots, when trying to escape imprisonment in Bolton Castle.

A land of castles and abbeys

Take the A6108 out of Leyburn and drive on to Middleham.

An important centre for horse breeding and training, Middleham is an attractive village. Yet it's perhaps better known for its huge Norman castle. Begun about 1170, it has a chequered history. Forfeited to the crown and Edward IV in 1471, he gave it to his brother, Richard of Gloucester, who later became Richard III. The 14th century church of St Mary and St Alkelda also has a fascinating history.

Four miles further on and we reach Jervaulx Abbey. The abbey is now in ruins, but the monks of this Cistercian abbey are credited with the creation of Wensleydale cheese.

I'm going to finish this particular tour by driving through East Whitton and onto Masham, for no other reason than it's here that we find the well-known Theakston's brewery, famous through the land for its 'Old Peculiar' beer. Tours around the brewery can be arranged, and needless to say there's the chance to try the odd sample or two.

If you have over imbibed, there's always the historic two-star Kings Head hotel for an overnight stay. You'll find it in the market square. ●

For our next outing, we'll be returning south to have a close-up look at the picturesque county of Hampshire.

East Whitton. It's early spring and the daffodils are putting on a show.

Enjoying your Jaguar

Trout streams and mellow thatch – Jerry Stamper takes us by Jaguar on another of his entertaining, yet relaxing, mini-tours to reveal some rich offerings in the south of England.

Part Six:
Hampshire

G646 parked outside one of the lovely cottages to be seen in Longparish – just one of the Test valley's chocolate-box villages.

W

e move south again for this, the sixth episode in our series. From the grandeur and wide sweeping scenery of North Yorkshire we travel to Hampshire. Cosy and intimate, there are many attractive villages, often clustered along the banks of gin-clear trout streams. In complete contrast, we also find the magnificent and historic New Forest, the biggest natural broad-leaf forest in Britain, covering most of the south of the county.

A Jaguar is at home touring in either habitat.

A chance find

My first introduction to the area was once again courtesy of the British Army. Stationed at the garrison town of Tidworth on the edge of Salisbury Plain, I was posted for a short time to a depot near the county town of Winchester.

Having packed my suitcase and loaded it onto the luggage rack of my 1949 MG TC sports car, I picked the most direct route I could find on the map. By chance, this was to introduce me to some stunning villages and a love affair with Hampshire that has lasted to this day.

A four-star start

Perhaps not the most picturesque part of the county, but we should start our mini-tour number six from Rotherwick near Basingstoke. The village itself has one or two eye-catching cottages, but for me it's the Tylney Hall hotel that must be Rotherwick's main claim to fame.

There just couldn't be a more pleasant place to treat yourself to a short stay. This four-red-star hotel is set in 66 acres of beautiful parkland, and the gardens that surround the Victorian country house were originally designed by Gertrude Jekyll. Among the sumptuous public rooms there is a wonderful oak-panelled dining room and the food served there is nothing short of superb.

Leaving Tylney Hall on the B3349 we travel south to pick up the A30 towards Basingstoke. However, it is best to take the ring road north to avoid the urban sprawl of this ever-developing town. From the A339 use

35

Enjoying your Jaguar
continued

Tylney Hall hotel in Rotherwick, near Basingstoke. A magnificent listed building, the hotel was used during the XK50 celebration Taste of England tour during 1998.

It's one way to earn a living. Jerry Stamper enjoying the peace and tranquillity of the stunning river Test. The footbridge is in the village of Wherwell, which straddles the river. Whichever way you turn there is another picture-postcard view.

the country lanes heading south to join the B3400 at Newfound. Here we turn right and make our way to Overton and Whitchurch.

Shoulder to shoulder

It's at Whitchurch that we enter the Test valley and follow the course of the river Test for some miles. Perhaps one of the most famous trout rivers in the country, the Test is stunning. At any number of beauty spots the clarity of its water enables you to see the trout sometimes almost shoulder to shoulder, simply holding station in its fast flowing current.

Whitchurch itself is interesting, and contains an 18th century silk mill, originally driven by water from the river. There is a shop selling various items of silk, along with other locally-made products.

A breathtaking experience

We stay on the B3400 until we reach Hurstbourne Priors, when we turn left to join the B3048. For the next five miles prepare yourselves for a feast of the most dazzling architecture to be found anywhere in England.

In particular, the village of Longparish is breathtaking. With every twist and turn in the road, you are confronted by another thatched cottage, each one seemingly prettier than the last.

Continue on the B3400 to the village of Wherwell. Here it's a must to find somewhere to park the car, and take in all that this delightful spot has to offer.

Quite simply stunning

The village could almost be a showroom for the art of thatching. The thatchers seem to have run riot – porches and windows are thatched and in places the roofs almost touch the ground. Even the tops of walls have received the same treatment!

As if this were not enough, Wherwell has a fascinating history. Next to the churchyard you'll find The Priory, an attractive 19th century house occupying the site of Wherwell Abbey. Dating back to

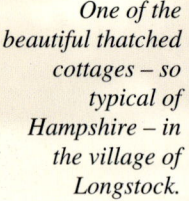
One of the beautiful thatched cottages – so typical of Hampshire – in the village of Longstock.

The parish church in Wherwell. It has a rather unusual spire made from wooden tiles.

Almost too much to take in. The village of Wherwell is simply breathtaking.

986, the Abbey was built for Queen Elfrida, mother of Ethelred the Unready, to make amends for the murder of her stepson, King Edward. Destroyed by fire during the dissolution of the Monasteries, fragments of the original building are still evident in the grounds of the house.

At the southern end of the village, next to a particularly attractive cottage called West Mill, look out for a small footpath leading down to the river. A narrow footbridge crosses the water, but I could just stand on the bridge for hours. The sound of the rushing water and the sight of the not insubstantial trout make for a hypnotic experience.

A fishy lunch stop

Continue to the end of the road, where we turn left to join the A3057. Half a mile further on you'll find The

Mayfly, a very popular pub, winter or summer. Nevertheless, get there a little early and it's well worth a visit. Excellent lunches are served and, if you sit outside by the river, try throwing a piece for bread into the water. The ducks will make a bee-line for it, but I'd lay even money that it will be snatched from below the water by a 2lb-plus trout, before the ducks get a look-in.

Leaving the pub, retrace your steps for a short distance before turning left and left again in the direction of Longstock and Stockbridge. As you cross the road-bridge the sight of the mill and millpond on the left is another stunner.

More pretty thatched cottages line the road into Stockbridge, another small town worth a stroll around. The architecture is mainly Victorian, but non-the-less attractive for all that. The river runs through the town and, incredibly, trout even inhabit this less attractive stretch of water.

Try taking the unclassified road south, through Houghton, and on to Mottisfont.

Roses grow on you

Here you will find Mottisfont Abbey. Owned by the National Trust, it is perhaps best known for its rose gardens. However, the 18th century Abbey houses a collection of paintings by Rex Whistler and incorporates the remains of the 12th century priory.

Leaving Mottisfont, pick up the A3057 and drive south to Romsey.

An ancient market town, Romsey has a good deal of charm and, at its centre, the splendid Norman abbey church. Just on its outskirts is Broadlands, the former home of Lord Mountbatten who lived here until his tragic death in 1979. The house has many connections with the Royal Family, and is best known as the honeymoon destination of both the Queen and The Duke of Edinburgh, and the Prince and Princess of Wales.

Broadlands itself is a wonderful example of 18th century architecture, the house and grounds being the work of 'Capability' Brown. In addition to the many works of art contained in the house, you'll find an exhibition of the distinguished life stories of Lord and Lady Mountbatten, with a 30 minute audio visual presentation of the *Life and Times of Lord Mountbatten*, all housed in the William and Mary stable block.

A truly great man, and a visit to his home is an absolute must.

A hunting we will go

It's here that we leave the Test valley, and make our way into the New Forest. We'll take the A3090 south to Cadnam, where we enter the forest proper.

I never tire of this area, and of all the places I've seen in both this country and abroad, I still feel that it's unique. Forests of oak and beech are so different to those of pine found on the continent, and somehow seem to have a special light.

However, it was not always the same. The ancient woodland was cleared for agriculture long before the Normans arrived on our shores. But it was William the Conqueror who, in 1079 laid claim to the land as a game reserve. So started a unique history, with the local inhabitants subject to special laws and ancient rights, many of which exist to this day. His son, the hot-tempered and often cruel William II, was killed by a stray arrow when hunting here in 1100.

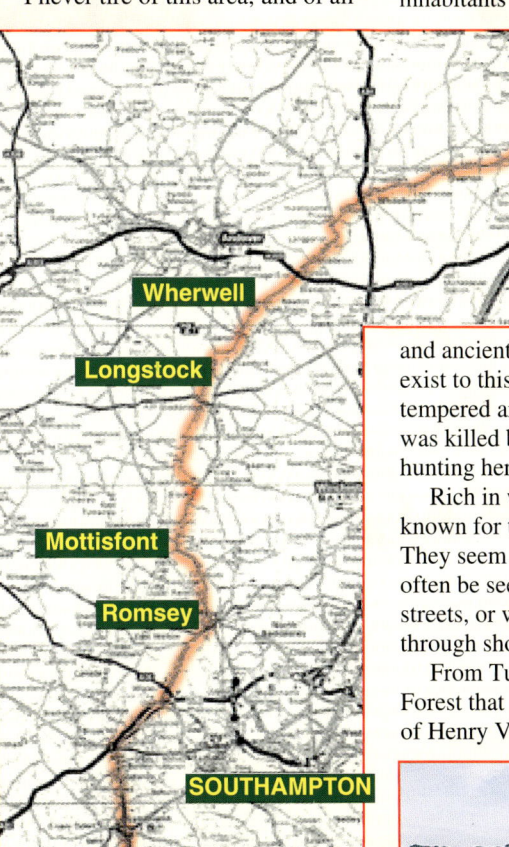

Rich in wildlife, the forest is well known for the New Forest ponies. They seem to amble at will, and can often be seen wandering in local high streets, or with their heads stuck through shop doorways.

From Tudor times it was the New Forest that supplied oak for the ships of Henry VIII, and shipbuilding

The main street of Bucklers Hard. Situated on the Beaulieu river, the street is wide enough for complete oak trees to be rolled down to the shipyard. It was here that many of Lord Nelson's ships were built.

Picture courtesy of the National Motor Museum, Beaulieu.

On the outskirts of Beaulieu village, overlooking the attractive river of the same name.

37

Enjoying your Jaguar
continued

continued at Bucklers Hard on the Beaulieu River until after Trafalgar.

We'll take the main A337 road from Cadnam to Lyndhurst. Popularly known as the capital of the New Forest, Lyndhurst is always busy, and its one-way system round the town can be a pain. But there's a large car park and plenty of places for lunch or a snack.

Continue on the A337 and a few miles further on you'll see the Balmer Lawn hotel on the left. It's here that we turn left and make our way to the country's motoring Mecca.

New Forest ponies enjoying the warm summer sunshine.

Just one small corner of the National Motor Museum at Beaulieu, showing part of that most wonderful collection of motor cars and motoring memorabilia.   Picture courtesy of the National Motor Museum, Beaulieu.

It will perhaps be worthwhile finding an overnight stopover for, barely a couple of miles away, situated on the Beaulieu River, you'll find Bucklers Hard. Again part of the Beaulieu Estate, it's another full day if you want to enjoy all there is on offer.

Great naval heritage
Bucklers Hard is quite simply unique. Nothing prepares you for the

Paying homage to our passion

The Palace House, home of Lord Montague of Beaulieu, has been synonymous with motoring since the turn of the century. The present Lord Montague's father had been a motoring pioneer and was in part responsible for introducing motoring to the Royal Family.

I well remember back in the late '50s, the small collection of cars housed in what appeared to be little more than a large shed. Today, the National Motor Museum has grown to what must be one of the most comprehensive displays of motoring history to be seen anywhere in the world. In addition to the cars there are many other attractions to make a memorable day out. The 'Wheels' exhibition is a particular favourite, taking you on a motorised journey through 100 years of motoring experience. As well as the motor museum, you will find the Palace House open to visitors, along with the original Cistercian Abbey of Beaulieu built by King John in 1204.

In the village, there is the Montague Arms hotel. Although only rated a three-star, both accommodation and food are of a particularly high standard.

Hampshire
Hotels

Tylney Hall	Rotherwick	01256 764881	Four-red-Star
Balmer Lawn	Lyndhurst	01590 623116	Three-star
The Montague Arms	Beaulieu	01590 612324	Three-star
The Master Builder	Bucklers Hard	01590 616253	Three-star
Chewton Glen	New Milton	01425 275341	Five-red-star

Some special local b&bs

Abbots Law, Abbots Ann, nr Andover.	01264 710350 (Apr - Oct)
Shearings, Rockbourne, nr Fordingbridge	01725 3256
Rudge House, nr Farnham	01252 850450
Yew Tree Farm, New Milton	01425 611041

The towns and villages
Rotherwick, Whitchurch, Longparish, Wherwell, Stockbridge, Mottisfont, Romsey, Lyndhurst, Beaulieu, Bucklers Hard, Lymington, New Milton

Places of interest

Mottisfont Abbey	April-Oct, Sat-Wed 12pm-6pm
	June only: Sat-Thur, noon-8.30pm
Romsey Abbey	Any time
Broadlands	April-Sept
	Mon-Thur 10am- 5.30pm
	Sat & Sun 10am-5.30pm
	August Fri only 10am-5.30pm
National Motor Museum	Daily. Easter-Oct 10am-6.00pm
	Oct-Easter 10am-5.00pm
Bucklers Hard	Daily. Easter-May 10am-6pm,
	June-Sept 10am-9pm
	Sept-Easter 10am-4.30pm
Sammy Miller Museum	Daily. All year 10am-4.30pm

sight of its main street which, in its day, must have been the widest to be found anywhere in England.

Having parked your car in the ample car park, you will be conducted to the small maritime museum. Here you will be introduced to the art of timber shipbuilding. For it was at Bucklers Hard that many great ships were built, all using the natural resource close at hand in the forest – British oak. Several of Lord Nelson's ships were built here, including the famous HMS *Agamemnon*.

From the museum you move on to the extraordinary Main Street. The buildings date from the 18th century and a number of them form part of the museum. Inside you'll find tableaus depicting the lives of the shipbuilders and their families.

At the bottom end of the main street, the house formerly occupied by the Master Ship Builder has been converted and extended into an attractive hotel called – appropriately enough – The Master Builder. It has a pleasant public bar, where good food and drink are served. Many of the hotel rooms overlook the beautiful Beaulieu River.

During the summer months a pleasure boat operates from the Hard, travelling down stream into the Solent, a very pleasing way to spend an hour or so on a warm summers day.

Something of a coincidence

From Bucklers Hard, we will take the smaller country lanes through the forest and on to Lymington. A particularly attractive little port, one of the Isle of Wight ferries operates from the quay across to Yarmouth. Originally known for its saltworks, which closed in the 19th century, Lymington is now famous as a yachting centre, and there are many restaurants in the town to suit all tastes and pockets.

Just on the outskirts of the town I chose *The White Hart*, a very pleasant pub for a lunch stop while taking the photographs for this article. Getting into conversation with Stuart Warren, the landlord, it turned out that he too owns an XJ40 very similar to mine and he, like me, loves the whole Jaguar experience. What could have been a rather solitary and boring lunchtime turned out to be a very pleasurable interlude.

The final leg

From Lymington it's only a short journey along the A337 into New Milton where, in Gore Road, you will find the Sammy Miller Museum. Accepted as one of the finest collections of interesting motor cycles, the museum has many machines that are the only surviving examples in the world. There are also many record-breaking bikes as well.

One of the finest hotels in the country is also to be found in New Milton – Chewton Glen, the only five-red-star hotel still in private hands. Built in the Palladian style, it was once the home of Captain Marryat, who wrote *Children of the New Forest* and *Mr Midshipman Easy*. Set in beautiful woodland and gardens, it has a health club with a most magnificent swimming pool.

Quite the best place to finish this particular mini tour. ●

For our next outing I'll be travelling to the east of the country visiting two counties which, for some reason, seem to be ignored. Yet they are steeped in history and have many hidden treasures. I speak of the beautiful 'Constable Country' of North Essex and South Suffolk. So join me soon for another in our series of 'Enjoying your Jaguar'.

'Wanna buy a new motor, John?' Lymington's yacht marina – now a mecca for yachtsmen – with some expensive-looking buys. The town itself is also attractive, with restaurants aplenty.

Stuart Warren, landlord of The White Hart *in Lymington, outside the pub with his pride and joy, a 1988 XJ40 Sovereign similar to my own. I spent a most pleasant lunchtime here.*

Nothing could better sum up the English countryside than these quaint thatched cottages with roses round the door – so typical of rural Hampshire.

39

Enjoying your Jaguar

My borrowed transport, a 1994 X-300 XJ6 3.2-litre Sovereign, resplendent in Anthracite black, parked just off the market square.

Le Talbooth restaurant, set on the banks of the River Stour, is reckoned to be one of the finest in East Anglia, if not the entire country.

40

Jerry Stamper suggests a mini-tour of the still beautiful 'Constable Country' as a 'short break' way to get more out of your Jaguar ownership.

Part Seven:
North Essex and south Suffolk

No doubt many of you have heard the odd 'Essex Girl' joke but, believe me, the urban sprawl of south Essex that seems an endless ribbon from East London all the way to Southend-on-Sea certainly isn't in any way funny.

Yet drive north to the other end of the county and you will find some of the most beautiful scenery anywhere in East Anglia.

The county border between Essex and Suffolk has of course become renown as the subject of many paintings by John Constable, *The Haywain* being perhaps the most reproduced.

Just to the south of East Bergholt, Flatford Mill and Willy Lott's cottage must be among the best known features in the east of England. However, we should not ignore the lesser-known but equally beautiful villages such as Thaxted, Finchingfield, Castle Hedingham and Stoke-by-Nayland, to mention just a few.

So, to adjust the balance, mini tour number seven will take us to some of the most stunning, but perhaps most ignored areas of our wonderful country.

A night in Dedham Vale

For an overnight stop, one of the most exceptional hotels in the area is to be found just outside the appealing village of Dedham. Overlooking Dedham Vale, the Maison Talbooth has a three-red-star rating and is a wonderful place to stay.

Unusually, the hotel's restaurant, Le Talbooth, is about half a mile away. So, it's either a gentle stroll or a courtesy car to drive you there. Set on the banks of the River Stour, the restaurant has a reputation for being one of the finest in England.

Although we will be visiting many attractive villages, we'll start this particular mini tour in the ancient town of Colchester.

Laying claim to being the oldest town in England, there is evidence of a settlement here dating back to the fifth century BC.

When the Romans invaded during 43 AD they chose Colchester as their capital, although it was to become a favourite for retiring legionnaires after London replaced it as the capital. Sacked by Boudicea in 60 AD, it was not

The village of Cavendish, with its pink washed cottages dwarfed by the tower of St. Mary's church.

The Bull Inn in Long Melford, just the job for a lunch stop.

Enjoying your Jaguar
continued

Always a feature of any English village is the church, and south Norfolk's are particularly grand having been endowed long ago by rich wool merchants. This is the church of Long Melford.

The imposing Norman keep of Hedingham Castle, built in the 12th century, it dominated the Colne Valley. (Photo by kind permission of the Hon. Thomas Lindsay)

until a thousand years later that the Normans invaded and built a huge fortress in the town. During the Civil War, Colchester faced a gruelling eleven-week siege, throughout which time its inhabitants ate practically everything that moved. The town finally surrendered and its Royalist leaders were executed. Much evidence of Colchester's turbulent past remains to this day.

Stepping into the picture

We'll leave Colchester north on the A12 and, after passing Stratford St Mary, look out for the signposts for a right turn to East Bergholt.

It was at East Bergholt that the painter John Constable was born, though it was the wool merchants of the Stour Valley that made the area famous long before Constable. Huge fortunes were made between the 13th and 16th centuries and the large number of stylish houses, and a magnificent church, are confirmation of that wealth.

Just a mile south of the village are Willy Lott's cottage and, straddling the River Stour there, Flatford Mill. There is a large car park and it's a short walk to visit these most famous landmarks. I feel I could write pages about this particular area, but would simply suggest that you try it for yourself.

Leaving Flatford Mill we drive back through East Bergholt, returning to the A12. Here we cross the road, picking up the B1068 through Higham, Thorington Street and on to Stoke-by-Nayland.

Dominated by the 15th century church of St Mary's, the village contains a number of fine examples of timber-framed Tudor houses, many of them virtually unchanged by the centuries. Inside the church you will find a brass memorial to Lady Howard, an ancestor of two of Henry VIII's ill fated wives, Catherine Howard and Anne Boleyn, both of whom were beheaded.

If you're here around lunch time then The Angel pub serves particularly good food, although it's very popular all year round, so you will need to get there early.

Let the train take the strain

Follow the B1087 west, crossing the A134 at Nayland and on to Burse. This attractive little town is full of fine half-timbered buildings.

If you have the relevant Ordnance Survey map find your way cross country via Cross End, Pebmarsh, Little Maplestead and Lucking Street to Castle Hedingham.

Now a sleepy little village, seemingly miles from anywhere, Castle Hedingham has a long and fascinating history. Dominated by the

One of the region's many 'wool' churches, in the village of Stoke-by-Nayland. There are many wonderful timber-framed houses to be seen here too.

The 3.2-litre Jaguar Sovereign parked in front of another quite beautiful timber framed house, this time on the outskirts of the small town of Thaxted.

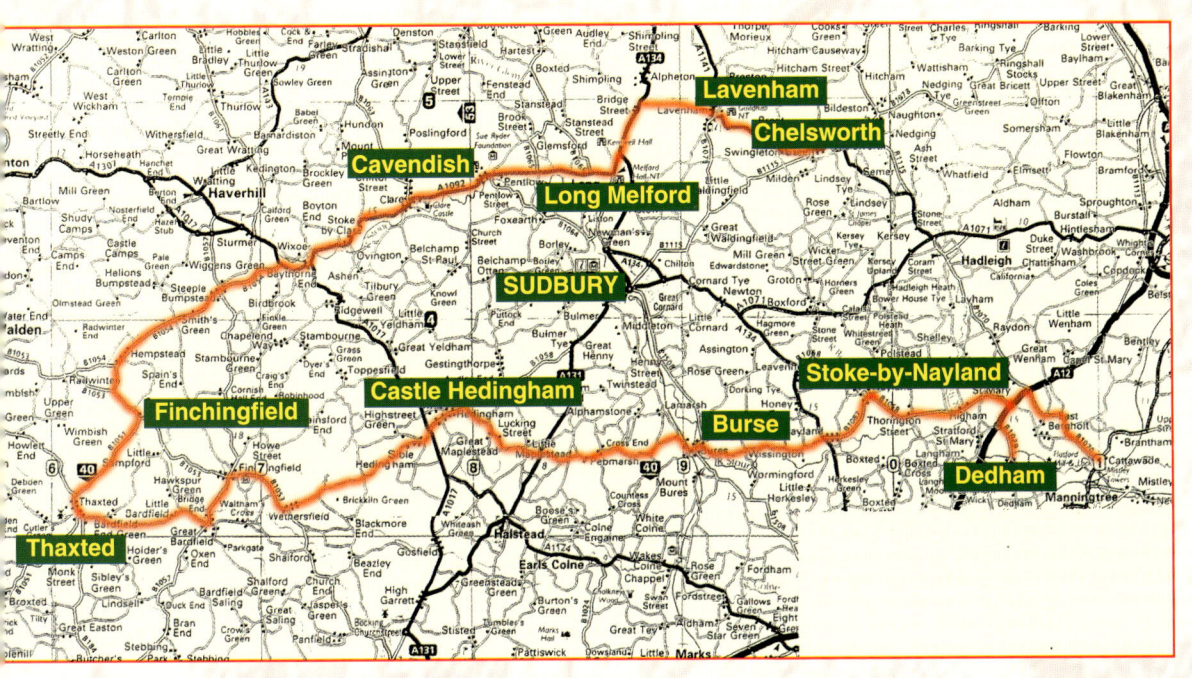

castle from which it gets its name, it was one of England's strongest fortresses in the 11th century.

It belonged to the powerful de Veres, the Earls of Oxford, one of whom was among the barons who forced King John to accept the Magna Carta. However, King John wrested the fortress from Robert de Vere in 1215.

It was during this period that Castle Hedingham was granted a market charter, and there are plenty of reminders of the days when this was a prosperous little town. The castle is open to the public, and the 12ft thick, 100ft high walls of its Keep are well worth a visit.

A short distance from the village on the A604, and well signposted, is the Colne Valley Railway & Museum. The railway buildings have been rebuilt, and with a wide range of steam locomotives, and other engines, carriages and wagons there is plenty to see and do. You can also travel in style in luxurious Pullman carriages that are used for a variety of social functions.

Quintessentially English

From Castle Hedingham, take the unclassified road south east, through Sible Hedingham and on to Wethersfield. Here we turn right on to the B1053 and drive into our next port of call.

Finchingfield is yet another striking village, and probably one of the most photographed in Essex. As you drive in, the village is spread below you, its green divided by the duck pond. It really is the archetypal English village. One particularly interesting building is the Fox Inn. Standing at the edge of the pond, the front of the building displays an especially fine example of the ancient art of 'pargetting', an attractive method of decorative exterior plastering, unique to this part of the country.

We leave Finchingfield, south on the B1057, to drive just two or three miles to another little gem. Great Bardfield is approached across a narrow stone causeway above beautiful water meadows.

The centre of the village is a mixture of half-timbered buildings, Georgian houses and shops. There is the 14th century church of St. Mary the Virgin, in which the organ case is said to be the work of Augustus Pugin, who designed the interior of the Houses of Parliament. To the east of the village standing out on the skyline is Gibraltar Mill, a wonderful tower windmill built in 1661.

Out-Sheffielding Sheffield

Turn right off the B1057 in the centre of Great Bardfield and follow the road through Little Bardfield. Continuing on you will reach the small town of Thaxted.

Now, I had always thought of Sheffield in Yorkshire as being the town that knives, forks and spoons came from, so it was something of a surprise to find that Thaxted grew prosperous as the centre of the cutlery trade during the 15th century. The cutlers' industry declined in the 16th century, possibly because of the shortage of trees on which they depended for fuel. However, at the bottom of Town Street stands the oak framed and plastered Cutlers Guildhall, which was built about 1400. The centre of the town is an extraordinary collection of medieval, Tudor and more modern architecture.

The wonderful church at the top of

The Colne Valley Railway and Museum. Well worth a visit.

The village green, complete with traditional village pond and noisy ducks, forms the centre of Finchingfield.

Enjoying your Jaguar
continued

A view across the fields towards Thaxted church and the windmill which is now a museum.

the street contains a chapel dedicated to John Ball, priest and martyr, who led the Peasants' Revolt in 1381.

The revolting peasants

We'll leave Thaxted, north on the B1051, turning left on to the B1053 at Great Sampford, with its attractive gabled houses and Elizabethan Manor House. A mile or so further on, turn right on the B1054 until you reach the main A1017, then left on the A1092 and drive into Stoke by Clare. This is another village that features buildings constructed between the 15th and 19th centuries. The church contains a wall painting, thought to be one of the last to be painted before the Reformation, and a short distance away there is a Tudor dovecote which belonged to a college of priests, who were transferred from a priory in Clare in 1124.

The ancient little market town of Clare is a few miles further along the A1092, where the remains of a Norman castle are to be found.

Lady Elizabeth Clare, who founded Clare College Cambridge during the 14th century, lived in the castle and the Augustinians founded their first priory in England here in 1248.

Staying on the A1092 the next village we come across is Cavendish, distinguished by its thatched cottages with pink-washed walls standing in front of the magnificent church of St Mary's. The name Cavendish comes from *Cafa's edisc*, an Anglo-Saxon settlement of 'Cafa's people' where *edisc* meant an 'enclosure'.

Sir John Cavendish was Chief Justice of the King's Bench, and was with Richard II in 1381 when he confronted Wat Tyler, leader of the Peasants' Revolt. Angered by the killing of their leader by Sir John's son, some of Tyler's supporters pursued Sir John to Cavendish, from where he fled to Bury St Edmunds. It was there he was later caught and beheaded.

The timber-framed Old Rectory built in the 16th century is now the headquarters of the Sue Ryder Foundation for the Sick and Disabled, and also houses a museum devoted to her work.

On the outskirts of the village you'll find Cavendish Manor Vineyards and Nether Hall. The 15th century manor is surrounded by vineyards, and tours and wine tasting are available.

A connection to Norfolk's great seafaring son

From Cavendish we continue east on the A1092, through Pentlow and on to Long Melford. Laid out along a former Roman road, Long Melford is steeped in history and tradition.

Worth a visit, the Bull Inn has an old galleried courtyard, where a murder was committed in 1648. The church is also worth seeing. On the east wall of the beautiful Lady Chapel there is a multiplication table, marked out during the 18th century, when it served as a school room.

Perhaps its most well-known landmark is Melford Hall, an imposing Elizabethan manor. Built around the time of the Dissolution of the Monasteries, it became the home of the Parker family during 1786. A distinguished seafaring family, it was to Sir Hyde Parker that Lord Nelson turned his blind eye when the order was given to break off the action at the Battle of Copenhagen in 1801.

A frequent guest and distant relative of the Parker family was the children's author Beatrix Potter, and a number of her water-colours are to be seen in the house.

Just a short distance north of the village is another mellow red brick Tudor mansion. Kentwell Hall built in the 16th century has a broad moat and beautiful gardens.

Simply outstanding

Part of the market square in the historic town of Lavenham. The Angel Inn hotel dates back to 1420.

From Long Melford we'll drive north to join the A134 and continue to the village of Bridge Street, where we turn right on the unclassified road and make our way to Lavenham, one of the most famous wool towns in East Anglia.

Devoid of television aerials and telephone wires, Lavenham has been uniquely preserved and is little changed since its heyday as one of the wealthiest wool towns during the 14th and 15th centuries. Practically every street contains a profusion of the most superb timber framed houses, their oak beams grey with age.

Set on the hillside and dominating

Town Street in Thaxted, with its attractive houses leading up to the church. Gustav Holst, the composer, lived in one of the houses between 1917 and 1925.

Looking more like a birthday cake, this cottage in Cavendish displays a magnificent example of 'pargetting', a method of decorating plaster walls, and unique to this part of the country.

The Guildhall in Lavenham. Now opened by the National Trust, it is perhaps one of the finest Tudor timber framed buildings in the country.

the town, the church of St Peter and St Paul has a 141ft flint tower and can be seen for miles around. It was endowed by wealthy merchants in thanksgiving for the end of the Wars of the Roses during 1485.

The market square looks much the same as it must have done during medieval times. Shilling Street runs off the square, though its name has nothing to do with money but comes from Schyling, one of several Flemish weavers imported to teach their skills to their English counterparts. From 1786 one of the street's most famous residents was the author and engraver Isaac Taylor, whose daughter Jane wrote the nursery rhyme *Twinkle, twinkle, little star*.

One of the finest Tudor half-timbered buildings in the country is the Guildhall, now a museum and owned by the National Trust.

If you are ready for an overnight stay there is the Forte Heritage Swan Hotel. Part of the old Wool Hall now forms some of this attractive hotel. A preserved section of one of the bars has initials carved by American servicemen of the 487th Bomber Group, who were stationed at a nearby airfield during the second world war.

Alternatively, there's the two-star Angel Inn in the market square whose history dates back to 1420 when it was first licensed. It's a popular spot with the locals, and both good food and beer are served.

Get out and walk?

Leaving Lavenham, we take the A1141 east to our final destination, the sleepy village of Chelsworth.

Any of the guidebooks will tell you that Chelsworth is best seen on foot. So, park the Jaguar and enjoy a stroll. Lacking the castles and mansions that we have seen in other villages during our mini tour, the variety of houses set alongside the babbling River Brett are little short of idyllic.

Indeed Chelsworth was the favourite of Julian Tennison, author of *Suffolk Scene* and great-grandson of the poet Alfred Lord Tennison. The village is noted for its gardens, and a number of them are open to the public on the last Sunday in June. ●

That concludes our seventh mini tour. Look out for something rather different when mini becomes maxi and join me on a drive through Belgium, Germany, Switzerland, France and then Italy, to spend time on stunning Lake Maggiore.

North Essex and south Suffolk

Hotels

Maison Talbooth	Dedham	01206 322367
The Rose & Crown	Colchester	01206 866677
The Swan Hotel	Lavenham	01787 247477
The Angel Inn	Lavenham	01787 247388

The villages
Dedham, Great Bardfield, East Bergholt, Thaxted, Stoke-by-Nayland, Stoke by Clare, Castle Hedingham, Clare, Finchingfield, Cavendish, Long Melford, Lavenham, Chelsworth.

Places of interest

Flatford Mill	A 'must see', but not open to the public.
Willy Lott's Cottage	Another 'must see', but again not open to the public.
St Mary's Church, Stoke-by-Nayland	Open any time.
Hedingham Castle	Apr-Aug, daily, except Fri, 11am-5pm, Sept-Oct Sat & Sun Only, Bank Hol Weekends and Good Friday.
Colne Valley Railway	All year, daily 10am till Dusk. For details of 'Steam Days' Tel: 01787 461174.
St Mary's Church, Great Bardfield	Open any time.
Sue Ryder Foundation	All year, daily 10am-5.30pm Closed 25th Dec.
Cavendish Manor and Nether Hall	All year, 11am-4.30pm.
Melford Hall	Apr: Sat and Sun, Bank Holiday Mon 2pm-5.30pm, May-Sept: Wed, Thur, Sat & Sun & Bank Holiday Mon, 2pm-5.30pm Oct: Sat & Sun 2pm-5.30pm.
Kentwell House	Tel: 01787 310207 for details and events.
Lavenham Guildhall	25 Mar-5 Nov: daily 11am-5.00pm.

Melford Hall, a beautiful red brick Tudor Manor. Queen Elizabeth I was a guest in 1578 and, in more recent times, Beatrix Potter often stayed here.

Enjoying your Jaguar

Bovington Tank Museum, and the X300 Sovereign is pictured in front of a Crusader tank, just one of over 300 exhibits in this superb museum.

The West Country
Jerry Stamper heads out west to explore some of the delights of Dorset and Somerset in this the first part of our Jaguar pilgrimage to the West Country.

It's a good few years since I ventured much past the Hampshire/Dorset border. So I was looking forward to renewing some dimly-remembered acquaintances, making this mini tour something of a pilgrimage.

With this in mind I chose the little, though busy, seaside resort of Lulworth in Dorset to start my journey. I first visited Lulworth and its famous cove nearly 40 years ago when stationed at the Royal Armoured Corps' gunnery ranges, part of which occupies a good deal of the cliff top area east of Lulworth. When not on duty, it was only a short walk into the attractive village, which was considerably quieter in those bygone days.

It was as a newly-married man that I made a second trip to this part of Dorset, and I still have vivid memories of an overnight stay at the *Castle Inn*. We pushed the two single beds in our hotel bedroom together, turning the sheets and blankets crossways, only for my wife and me to disappear down the gap in the middle during a night of unbridled passion. But that's another story! The *Castle Inn* is still there and serves a very good lunch.

There are also a couple of two-star hotels in West Lulworth, the *Shirley* and the *Cromwell House*, and of course any number of comfortable B&Bs to stay in.

Continuing the military theme

We leave Lulworth on the B3071 and drive north to the village of Wool, where we turn right over the level crossing on to the A352 and follow the signs to Bovington. Bovington Camp is the headquarters of the Royal Armoured Corps and in the village itself there is the world-renowned Tank Museum.

There are well over 300 vehicles to see, and the museum gives a dramatic insight into the lives and living conditions of tank soldiers since the first tank saw action in 1916. During the summer months there are regular action days, where visitors can take a ride on a tank.

Turn right out of the museum and a short distance further up the road you will find Clouds Hill. Now in the hands of the National Trust, it was once the home of T E Lawrence ('Lawrence of Arabia') who bought the cottage in 1925 when he was a private in the Tank Corps at Bovington. From the car park the walk to the cottage is via a pathway through the most magnificent rhododendrons. Every year during late May and early June they are at their best and look utterly stunning.

Turn right out of Clouds Hill car park and at the T-junction turn left and follow the unclassified roads through Pallington, Tincleton and Ilsington, taking the second turning on the right into Higher Bockhampton, famous as the birthplace of Thomas Hardy. The surrounding countryside provides the landscape of his books – known as Wessex – and the nearby County town of Dorchester appears in his novels as 'Casterbridge'.

Dorchester is perhaps worth a visit, being the scene of Judge Jefferies and his 'Bloody Assizes' in 1685 and the trial of the Tolpuddle Martyrs in 1834. However, we will

The Castle Inn in Lulworth serves a good lunch, and was the scene of some 'nocturnal high jinks' in Jerry's younger days.

Adjacent to Lulworth Cove are these spectacular limestone cliffs, formed by years of sea erosion.

Bovington Tank Museum in Dorset has a collection of over 300 tanks, and includes special displays giving a graphic account of the life of a tank soldier since the tank first appeared in 1916.

A riverside cottage in the attractive village of Piddlehinton. It gets part of its name from the river Piddle.

The Cerne Abbas 'Giant'. Cut into the chalk hill, this 180ft figure pre-dates the Romans and is believed to be associated with fertility rights. I can't think why!

Montacute House, a wonderful Tudor mansion. This is just the gatehouse.

Typical honey-coloured stone cottages on the outskirts of Stoke sub Hamdon. The building material is quarried locally at Ham Hill.

Built between 1590 and 1604 Montacute House was owned by Sir Phelips, a successful lawyer. An immense 189ft gallery runs the entire length of the second floor.

Enjoying your Jaguar continued

stick to the minor roads. Leaving Higher Bockhampton continue north the short distance to the A35.

Here we join the A35 east, signposted Poole & Puddletown, and drive for a couple of miles before forking left on to the A354 and then at the roundabout left to join the B3142 at Puddltown.

Piddle in the Puddle

We'll drive north on the B3142 through the wonderfully-named villages of Piddlehinton and Piddletrenthide, both getting their names from the nearby river Piddle, or more politely the river Trent. It's worth parking the car in Piddlehinton and taking a walk through the village. The picturesque thatched cottages with the river close by are almost out of this world.

Continue to Piddletrenthide where we take a left turn and follow the unclassified roads to the charming village of Cerne Abbas. It's full of stunning Tudor cottages and Abbey ruins, along with a number of excellent pubs. Two in particular are the *Red Lion* and the *Royal Oak*, both in Long Street and both mentioned in *The Good Pub Guide*. A leisurely walk round the village is another must.

However, Cerne Abbas is probably best known for its Giant, administered by the National Trust. This 180ft figure is cut into the chalk hillside and is believed to be associated with fertility rights and to date back to pre-Roman times.

From here we take the A352 north towards Sherbourne. This section of road is particularly attractive; it's a great road to drive and the views are

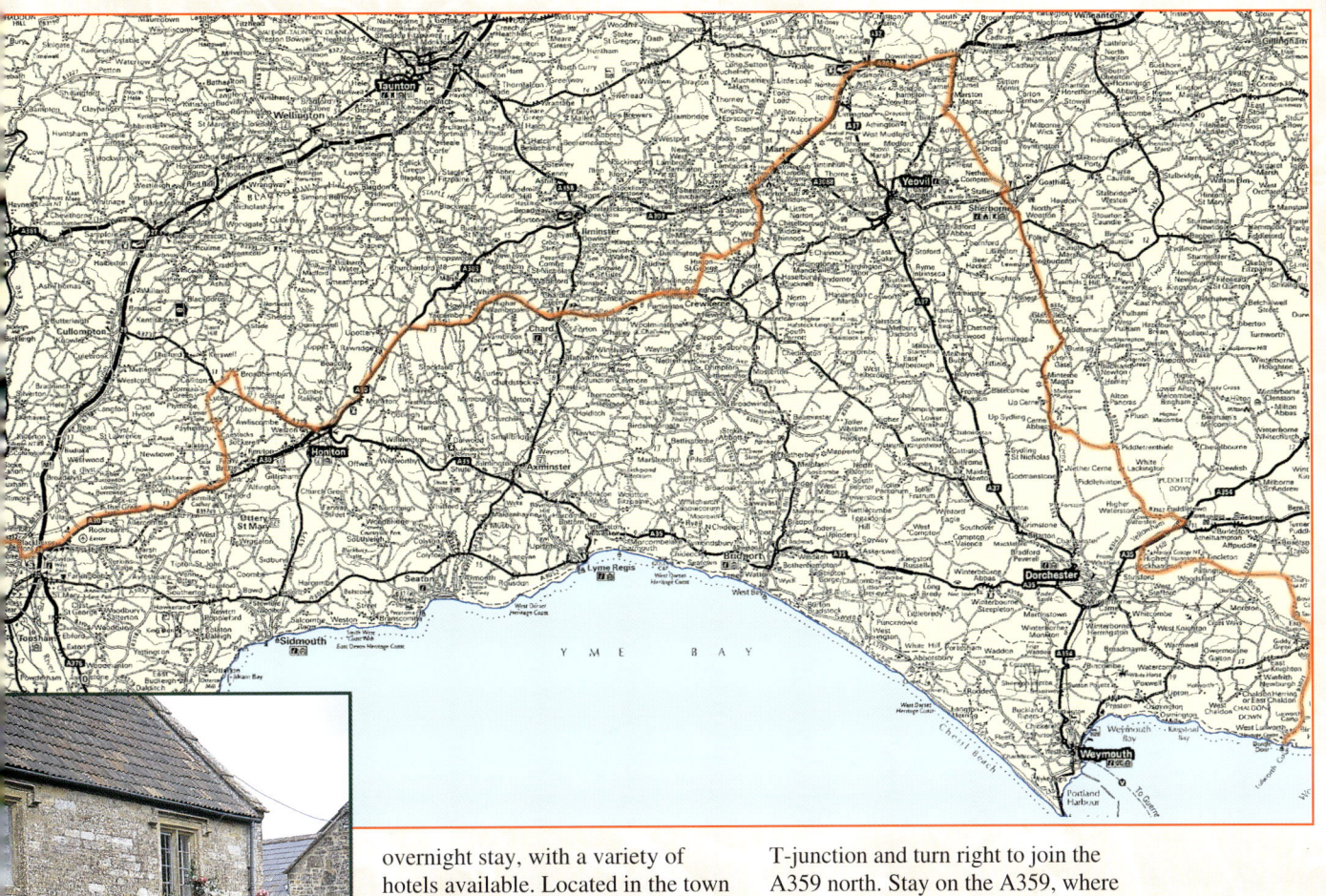

The quintessential English cottage with roses round the door. Just one of the many attractive houses in the village of Montacute.

simply breathtaking. The quaint town of Sherbourne is steeped in history, with perhaps its most well-known resident being Sir Walter Raleigh. Queen Elizabeth 1 first leased and then eventually gave him the 12th century Old Castle, which is now open to the public daily.

It's quite a reasonable size town and makes an ideal place for an overnight stay, with a variety of hotels available. Located in the town centre there's the *Eastbury* and the *Antelope* hotels both of which are three-star. Moving on from Sherbourne we pick up the main A30, and then find the B3148.

Continue north until you reach a T-junction and turn right to join the A359 north. Stay on the A359, where after a couple of miles or so you will reach a large roundabout at the junction with the A303. Here we follow the signs to Sparkford and our next destination, the superb Haynes Motor Museum.

Outside the Haynes Motor Museum. John Haynes OBE (right of picture) with the magnificent, newly-acquired XJ220. With him are Chris Haynes, the museum's Development Manager, and Michael Penn, the Curatorial Director.

49

A lovely terrace of thatched cottages in the village of Hinton St George.

Enjoying your Jaguar continued

An unrivalled collection

The Haynes Motor Museum is the brainchild of John Haynes OBE, Chairman of the Haynes Group, the publishers of the highly-regarded Haynes Manuals. The motor museum was opened in 1985.

Since then it has grown to be one of the largest and most varied collections of motor vehicles and motoring memorabilia in the UK. In addition to the museum, which is currently being extended to include the new Millennium Hall, there is a free Video Cinema, Vehicle Display Track and a cafe and picnic area. There are many other attractions to entertain the enthusiast and a visit is highly recommended. John Haynes himself is a passionate owner of several Jaguars, and *Jaguar Monthly* has been proud to welcome him and his wife Annette on a number of our tours.

Easily overlooked

Assuming you're able to tear yourself away, we return to the A303 and head towards Devon.

Needless to say, the most direct route into Devon, our third county to be visited, is straight along the A303. But why not make a change? Within half a mile of this major trunk road are stunning villages like Stoke sub Hamdon, Montacute and Hinton St George, to name just three.

To the south of Stoke sub Hamdon is Ham Hill. Now a country park, it contains evidence of prehistoric fortifications and of centuries of quarrying for the honey-coloured stone used to build the attractive 17th century houses and cottages. There is also a 14th century priory now maintained by the National Trust.

Montacute is dominated by Montacute House, a magnificent Elizabethan mansion. With a history dating back over 1,000 years it makes a village of exceptional interest. Hinton St George is another village built of golden stone. Seat of the Poulett family, it is said that Sir Amyas Poulett had the future Cardinal Wolsey put in the stocks for being drunk and disorderly when he was a young parish priest.

In the centre of the village you'll find *The Lord Poulett* – a 17th century inn. Its rather grand exterior somewhat belies its interior, which is a mixture of black painted beams and bare masonry walls. Yet the beer is extremely good. Try a pint of Butcombe Bitter and you'll see what I mean. The food is pretty good too.

Jerry's X300 Sovereign parked in the remarkable village of Hinton St George.

Something of a dilemma

To make the most of some smashing scenery we leave Hinton St George via South Street and drive a few miles to join the A30, turning right towards Chard.

The roads on this part of the journey are naturally fairly well used, yet the scenery and sweeping bends make up in every way for the slight inconvenience.

As we travel further west names like Taunton, Honiton, Ilminster and particularly Exeter seem to revive memories of mammoth traffic jams, cars at the roadside with bonnets up and steam rising from boiling engines. Although it has been some years since I travelled these roads, I am sure the M4 and M5 have improved the situation no end. Yet without travelling a most convoluted route, we'll unfortunately have to tackle the busy Exeter by-pass before travelling further west.

The main road in Broadhembury. The village is situated five miles north of Honiton. Augustus Montague Toplady was the vicar of St Andrews church in 1768.

Nonetheless, before we do, the village of Broadhembury just off the A373 five miles north west of Honiton is well worth a look and, indeed, it's almost a step back in time. Dedicated in 1259, the church of St Andrews overlooks the village square, with many of its stunning thatched cottages dating back to the 16th century. One of the memorials in the church is to the writer of the hymn *Rock of Ages*, a gentleman who was called Augustus Montague Toplady and was the vicar of Broadhembury from 1768.

Park your car in the broad village square and take the short walk up to the church, from the side door there is a view across the churchyard that will take your breath away.

Peace and tranquillity in the hamlet of Broadhembury in Devon.

And finally

I am going to conclude our journey in Exeter. Like so many towns, Exeter is often thought of as an obstacle on route to somewhere else. However, it is certain worth staying overnight. There is, as you might expect, accommodation aplenty, from the four-star *Southgate*, to the two-star *Fairwinds Hotel*.

Exeter was founded by the Romans at the lowest crossing point of the river Exe, and is one of the oldest cities in England. Parts of the old Roman city walls are still evident today, but much of the medieval Exeter was, sadly, destroyed during the Second World War. Its magnificent cathedral of course dominates the town. The 300ft nave has the longest span of Gothic vaulting in the world. Luckily, this wonderful building and the attractive old houses round the close were spared the bombing.

In addition to its Roman history, there is the marvellous Maritime Museum, and the Guildhall, which make the city of Exeter a place of very special interest.

Aside from the wonderful scenery, which will leave you breathless in many places, my overwhelming memory of Dorset and Somerset is the excellent driving roads, where a Jaguar really does come into its own.

The Hotels

Shirley Hotel	two-star	West Lulworth	01929 400358
Cromwell Hotel	two-star	West Lulworth	01929 400253
Eastbury Hotel	three-star	Sherbourne	01935 813131
Antilope Hotel	three-star	Sherbourne	01935 812077
Southgate Hotel	four-star	Exeter	01392 412812

Places of interest

Bovington Tank Museum
    Open all year daily 10am - 5pm. Closed over Christmas.
Clouds Hill   Open 2 April-29 October, Wednesday-Friday,
    Sunday and Bank Holiday Monday, 2pm - 5pm.
Haynes Motor Museum
    Open all year daily 9.30am - 5.30pm.
    Closed 25/26 December and 1 January.
Sherbourne Old Castle
    Open April-September daily 10am-6pm.
    October 10am-4pm.
    November-March Wednesday-Sunday 10am-4pm.

ENJOYING YOUR JAGUAR

The Thames

We join Jerry Stamper on a very foggy day, as he takes us on a delightful tour of the Thames Valley.

Pics: Mike Key

It was the poet John Burns who described the Thames as 'liquid history', and indeed it was the Thames that gave birth to London – the nation's capital.

However, for this mini tour we'll avoid London and start our journey through the Thames Valley from the town with the largest inhabited castle in the world – Windsor. Following the course of the Thames, we'll make our way west towards Oxford and beyond.

I got to know this particularly attractive part of England during the time I was selling office equipment and the Thames Valley formed part of my 'patch'. Needless to say I wasted a good deal of selling-time exploring some of the many beauty spots the area has to offer.

The numerous palaces, castles, country houses, unique villages and other places of interest bear testament to the fact that much of the country's history has been lived and worked along this most famous of rivers.

Windsor is on the list of every tourist who visits England and, not

alley

ENJOYING YOUR JAGUAR — The Thames Valley

Start point for our tour of the Thames Valley. Windsor Castle is the largest inhabited castle in the world.

Built in 1831 the suspension bridge at Marlow is one of the most attractive on the Thames. We chose a misty morning, but the XKR looks good in any setting.

unexpectedly, is very busy all year round. Nevertheless, the castle makes a spectacular sight and dominates the town.

Also well worth a visit is the Household Cavalry Museum, reckoned to be one of the finest military museums in the country. If you cross the footbridge at the end of Thames Avenue in Windsor village you could round off the day with a look at Eton College and its gothic chapel.

Oddly, there is not a huge choice of hotel accommodation in the town, but if you want to give yourself a bit of a treat there's the four-star gothic Victorian, *Oakley Court* hotel situated on the banks of the river.

The Vicar of Bray Sir

Leave Windsor on the A308 in the direction of Maidenhead, and after the motorway bridge turn right on to the B3028 and into the village of Bray.

Made famous by the song *The Vicar of Bray*, this Thameside village has some particularly eye-catching almshouses founded by William Goddard in 1627. Little more than a mile further on is the town of Maidenhead, a mixture of old and new in architectural terms, the smart and expensive riverside houses are popular with many television personalities. Indeed, I am told that well-known names like Terry Wogan, Michael Parkinson and Carol Vorderman are regularly seen at the local supermarket. And that Saturday mornings are the best times for name spotting.

Cross the bridge to the north side of the river and turn right, to follow the signs for Boulters Lock. This typical Thames lock is always busy and has been the subject of numerous artists since Victorian times. There is an excellent little hotel behind the lock, and if you walk past the hotel and across a footbridge, you'll find yourself on Boulters Island. A smashing little spot, particularly up by the weir, and a place where I had numerous picnics when I was a child.

Leave Maidenhead on the A308 and continue until you reach a roundabout at the junction with the A404. Crossing the A404, follow the sign posts to Bisham. Just before entering the village, on the left you will find Bisham Abbey. This beautiful 800-year-old abbey sits on the banks of the Thames and was formerly the home of the Knights Templars. It is now one of the National Sports Centres, and is often used by the England football team for training sessions. I had the pleasure of staying there for a week-long residential badminton coaching course some years ago when I was a good bit slimmer and a whole lot fitter. However, it is certainly a most beautiful location.

Drive through the little village of Bisham and on to the town of Marlow. Just before you cross the suspension bridge built in 1831, you'll find the internationally famous four-star *Complete Angler Hotel*, named after the fishing book by Izaak Walton.

Marlow itself is a pleasant mixture of 16th, 17th and 18th century buildings, and has many literary connections. Percy Bysshe Shelly and his wife Mary lived there for a while, and it was here that Mary wrote *Frankenstein*. T S Elliot lived just down the road, and Jerome K Jerome wrote some of *Three Men In A Boat* in the *Two Brewers* pub in St Peters Street.

Hell, fire and damnation

Continue up the High Street to the roundabout and turn left onto the A4155, signposted Henley. The road winds through attractive tree-lined scenery with occasional glimpses of the river. Lying halfway between Marlow and Henley is the village of Medmenham. Turn left in the village and the narrow cottage-lined road leads down to a particularly beautiful stretch of the river. Some years ago my wife and I were fortunate enough to have a friend who owned one of the cottages, and we spent a few wonderful weekends in this idyllic village.

Its main claim to fame arose during the 18th century when Sir Francis Dashwood rebuilt the Norman abbey in which to hold meetings of his notorious Hellfire Club.

Return to the A4155, and turn left to make your way to one of the Thames valley's most well-known towns – Henley-on-Thames.

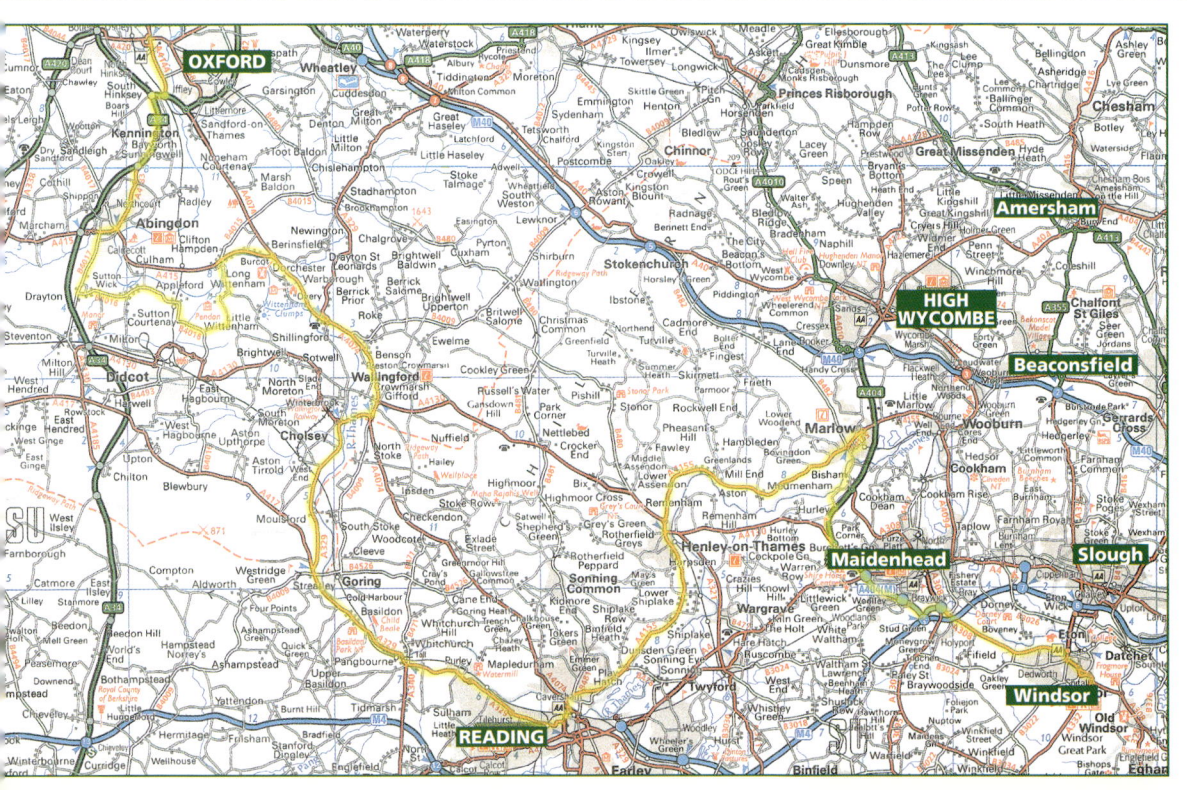

World-renowned for its annual Royal Regatta held during July, needless to say there is plenty of boating available during the summer months. The town centre itself has numerous shops, teashops and inns, but perhaps the favourite pastime is simply walking along the towpaths, watching the world go by.

Once again we join the A4155 to travel south in the direction of Reading. At the *Flowering Spring* pub turn left to pick up the B478 and drive into another riverside gem – Sonning. Quiet and unspoilt, the river seems to be everywhere with an 18th century bridge consisting of 11 arches spanning the water. A mixture of pretty cottages and Georgian houses make up most of the village

Bisham Abbey. One of the country's finest sports centres. The ultra modern facilities are tucked away in the magnificent grounds, in complete contrast to the 800 year old Abbey.

My wife and I had the pleasure of staying in this stunning cottage on a number of occasions. It's in the village of Medmenham, made famous by Sir Francis Dashwood when he rebuilt the Norman abbey where he held meetings of his notorious Hellfire Club.

55

ENJOYING YOUR JAGUAR The Thames Valley

Truly a season of mists and mellow fruitfulness, the churchyard in the village of Sonning looks superb in late autumn.

Whitewashed cottages in the lovely village of Sonning.

nd there is a watermill that is currently used as a theatre. Altogether a charming little hamlet, and one not to be missed.

For our next port of call, we return to the A4155 and head for Caversham. Just before Caversham Bridge turn right onto the A4074 and follow the signs for Mapledurham House.

Mapledurham House, still the home of the descendants of the original family, is an Elizabethan manor house idyllically situated beside the Thames and sheltered by the Chiltern Hills. There has also been a mill on the site since Saxon times and the present building dates from the 15th century, making it the only surviving working watermill on the Thames.

The village itself was chosen by John Galsworthy as the site for Soames Forsyte's country house in *The Forsyte Saga*.

Travelling on we rejoin the A4074 and find our way to Pangbourne. A pleasant enough town, Kenneth Graham (author of *Wind in the Willows*) lived and died here, and it is here that we turn north to follow the river towards Oxford.

Take the A329 in the direction of Wallingford. This is a particularly attractive stretch of road with the river on your right. There are any number of tranquil riverside pubs at which to while away an hour or so. Continue along the road until you reach the village of Streatley. Turning right in the middle of the village will take you down to the river and on the opposite side you will find the village of Goring and Goring Lock.

Leave the car and walk

It really is worth parking the car and having a wander round this lovely area. Goring is the larger of the two riverside villages and is full of Edwardian buildings and quaint pubs. It is here that the river Thames separates the Chilterns from the Berkshire Downs, through the Goring Gap. The prehistoric Icknield Way, part of the Ridgeway, crosses the river where a ferry existed until a bridge was built about 100 years ago. On the Streately side of the river you will find the excellent four-star *Swan Diplomat* hotel (once owned by the entertainer Danny La Rue). Just the place for a relaxing lunch, though if you stay overnight make sure you get a room with a balcony which overlooks the river, even if you have to pay a little extra. All the public rooms have wonderful views, and during the summer months the terrace is the place to waste a few hours.

From Streatley we continue north on the A329. Stay on the 329 through the busy town of Wallingford and at Shillingford turn left onto the A423. Shortly

The car park of The Swan *pub on the road from Pangbourne to Streatley. One of my favourite lunch time stopping points – and with this view, is it any wonder?*

The four star Swan Diplomat *hotel at Streatley on Thames, with its original Oxford Barge moored close by. The barge is used for private functions. The hotel itself was once owned by female impersonator Danny La Rue.*

Goring Lock. It is here that the Thames separates the Chilterns from the Berkshire Downs, the famous Goring Gap. It's well worth a walk round the village.

afterwards bear left to take the minor road into Dorchester. Now a town of little significance, it has a long and fascinating history. It was in 634 AD that the Saxons built a cathedral that was the headquarters of a dioceses which stretched as far as North Yorkshire. Following the Norman conquest an Augustinian abbey was founded in 1170 and built on the cathedral site. A walk round the fascinating cobbled high street and little lanes is well worth the effort.

Leaving Dorchester, drive north through Burcot and on to Clifton Hampden, a village of half timbered and thatched cottages. The *Barley Mow Inn*, also made famous in Jerome K Jerome's book *Three Men In A Boat*, stands by the bridge. Cross the bridge and follow the unclassified road through Long Wittenham and Little Wittenham, both attractive villages. There's an interesting museum called the Pendon in Long Wittenham. The B4016 will take you on to Sutton Courtney, reckoned to be one of the most beautiful villages on the Thames. In the churchyard can be found the graves of the author George Orwell, and former Prime Minister Lord Asquith.

Driving on along the B4016, turn right at Drayton, joining the B4017 and going on to the town of Abingdon. Once the county town of Berkshire it now lies within the boundary of Oxfordshire. Its main claim to fame as far as the motoring fan is concerned is that for many years it was the home of the MG Car Company.

Dreaming spires

We'll round off this particular mini tour by driving north to the university city of Oxford, where there is so much to see and do you could comfortably spend two or three days there.

Oxford University actually consists of 35 separate colleges, the oldest of which dates back to the 12th century. Of course, Oxford is far more than just the university. Indeed the major part of the town became prosperous as a result of the motorcar industry, and it was at nearby Cowley that Britain's first mass-produced cars appeared in the 1920s.

On the list of places to visit, Christ Church College is Oxford's largest and most prestigious, then there are the Ashmolean Museum, the Museum of Oxford and the Bodleian Library, to mention just a few.

Should you want to really pamper yourself you might want to spend a night at the famous *Le Manoir Aux Quat' Saisons*, a hotel and restaurant run by Raymond Blanc. Situated just a few miles south east of Oxford at Great Milton, this 15th Century manor house has a reputation second to none.

Don't forget that Oxford is the eastern gateway to the beautiful Cotswolds, and we have covered those in earlier issues of *Jaguar Monthly*.

Hotels

Oakley Court, Windsor	4-star	01753 609988
Complete Angler, Marlow	4-star	01628 484444
Swan Diplomat, Streatley-on-Thames	4-star	01491 878800
Le Manoir Aux Quat' Saisons, Great Milton	4-red star	01844 278881

Places of interest

	Open
Windsor Castle	All year daily (subject to closure at short notice)
Household Cavalry Museum	All year Mon-Fri 9am-12.30pm and 2pm-4.30pm
Mapledurham House	Easter-Sept, Sat, Sun and bank holidays – 1pm-5pm
Christ Church College	Most afternoons
Ashmolean Museum	All year Tue-Sat 10am-4pm. Sun 2pm-4pm
Museum of Oxford	All year Tue-Fri 10am-4pm. Sat 10am-5pm
Bodleian Library	All year

KELSEY BOOKS

A series of books based on some of the best articles reprinted from some of the leading motoring magazines. Each one a definitive work in its own right.

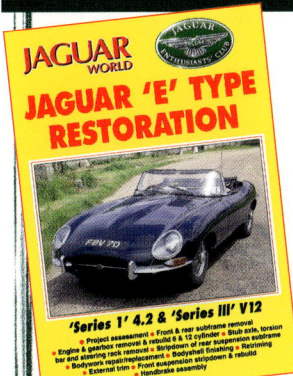

Jaguar World / Jaguar Enthusiast
Jaguar E-Type Restoration

Comprehensive restoration guide using a Series 1 roadster and Series 3 fixed head. A4, 108 pages, mostly in colour.

£17.95 inc p&p (UK)

Jaguar Monthly / Car Mechanics
Jaguar XJ40

The first ever step-by-step buying, maintenance and restoration guide to the XJ40. A4 format, softbound, 120 pages, plus covers, full-coloured throughout, highly illustrated – over 520 photos!

£17.95 inc p&p (UK)

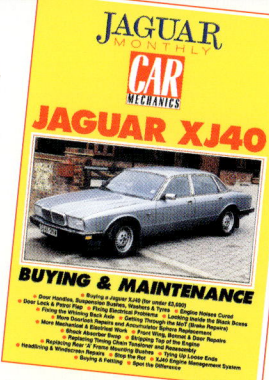

Jaguar World
Jaguar 6-Cylinder Engine Overhaul (1948-1986)

The most in-depth coverage of a rebuild on this engine, including IRS and SU carburettors. A4, 96 pages, many in colour.

£14.95 inc p&p (UK)

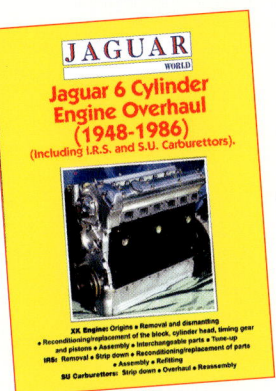

Practical Classics
Mk2 Jaguar Restoration

Highly-detailed step-by-step DIY restoration. The only work of its kind on this model. A4, over 100 pages, mostly in colour.

£16.95 inc p&p (UK)

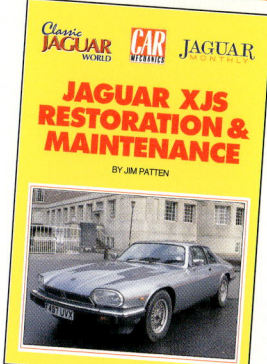

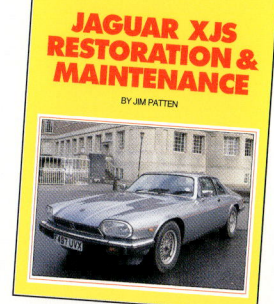

Classic Jaguar World / Jaguar Monthly
XJS Restoration

The essential guide for restoration of Jaguar's popular XJS. A4, xxx pages, all in colour.

£17.95 inc p&p (UK)

Jaguar Enthusiast
Jaguar/Daimler XJ6 Restoration

The most detailed step-by-step DIY restoration coverage ever undertaken on an XJ6 Jaguar. A4, 128 pages and over 450 illustrations, mostly black and white with some colour pages.

£16.95 inc p&p (UK)

Practical Classics
Jaguar E-Type Restoration CD

The original 'Practical Classics' 100+ page book (now out of print) has been placed on an easy-to-follow CD! All the same clear colour and black and white (mostly colour illustrations (over 300) and text as the original book. Includes the 'Series' evolutionary changes.

£17.95 inc p&p (UK)

Jaguar Enthusiast
Jaguar XK120 Restoration

The most comprehensive restoration guide ever undertaken on any model, includes chassis, bodywork, engine etc. A4, 128 pages, profusely illustrated, mostly in colour.

£18.95 inc p&p (UK)

Please allow 14 days delivery
Post coupon to: Kelsey Books Dept, Kelsey Books, Cudham Tithe Barn, Berrys Hill, Cudham, Kent TN16 3AG.
Tel: 01959 541444 *(Mon-Fri 9.00am – 5.30pm).* Fax: 01959 541400
E-mail: books@kelsey.co.uk

Kelsey Books
Please send me:
Jaguar E-Type Restoration
 at **£17.95** (inc p&p) ❏
Jaguar XJ40 Buying and Maintenance
 at **£17.95** (inc p&p) ❏
Jaguar 6-Cylinder Engine Overhaul
 at **£14.95** (inc p&p) ❏
Mk2 Jaguar Restoration at **£16.95** (inc p&p) ❏
Jaguar/Daimler XJ6 Restoration
 at **£16.95** (inc p&p) ❏
Jaguar XK120 Restoration at **£18.95** (inc p&p) ❏
XJS Restoration at **£17.95** (inc p&p) ❏
Jaguar E-Type Restoration CD
 at **£17.95** (inc p&p) ❏
**FOR OVERSEAS, PLEASE ADD:
£4 PER BOOK SURFACE MAIL, £6 AIRMAIL.**

I enclose my cheque for £ .... *(payable to Kelsey Publishing Ltd)*
(Or) I wish to pay by:
Mastercard ❏ Visa ❏ Switch ❏ Amex ❏
Card no.: ....
Expiry date: .... Switch issue no.: ....
Signature: ....
Name: ....
(BLOCK CAPITALS PLEASE)
Address: ....
....
....
Post code: .... Day tel no: .... JM

ENJOYING YOUR JAGUAR

Derbyshire

Jerry Stamper takes a voyage of discovery around the delightful countryside of the Peak District.

Pics: Mike Key

The Peak District offers a wonderful combination of great driving roads, mesmerising scenery and charming villages and towns that are well worth a visit. My knowledge of this area is less than that of many other parts of the UK, so I was looking forward to finding out more about it. But there was another reason for my excitement about probing around the Peak District.

Instead of my own XJ6 4.0-litre Sovereign, I was going to complete the trip in a stunning new XKR. Sadly, as the pictures will show, the weather during our trip (in early March) could not have been more unkind.

A questionable choice

If you're going to visit the area you may choose, as we did, to make the elegant town of Buxton your base. There are a number of hotels in the town, with the four-star Palace Hotel being the largest and most well known.

We chose a bed and breakfast on the Internet, and, boy, did we make a mistake! It was like something from the 1950s. For those of you who remember the film *Genevieve*, the place reminded me of the hotel run by Joyce Grenfell, with the old fashioned reception, hand-written notices everywhere and a level of service that

Peak District

Glorious Georgian architecture. The Crescent in Buxton sets off the striking curves of the 370bhp XKR.

ENJOYING YOUR JAGUAR

On the road from Chapel-en-le-Frith to Glossop and an old mill near the village of Hayfield.

proper. From here the road starts to rise steeply, twisting and turning its way to the aptly named 'Snake Pass'. When we did the trip, we stopped near the top, but for us what surely would have been the most magnificent of views were totally obscured by cloud and heavy mist.

As the road descends in the direction of Sheffield there are numerous fissures in the vast rock faces, where attractive waterfalls tumble towards the valley.

A few miles further on, we reach the vast waters of the Ladybower Reservoir. Labybower is the largest of a chain of three massive reservoirs collectively known as the 'Peakland Lake District'. Howden and Derwent Dams lie further up the valley. They were used by the wartime RAF's 617 Squadron in their training with Barnes Wallis' 'bouncing bomb', and much of the film *The Dambusters* was filmed there. We seemed geared to the convenience of the proprietor.

I should just name and shame the place, but let's just say that it had the same name as a famous London hotel situated on Park Lane.

Buxton itself is a wonderful example of a Georgian spa town, with beautifully proportioned buildings, an opera house and the magnificent Pavilion Gardens. It also has the reputation of being the highest town in England, although I believe that Stow-on-the-Wold in the Cotswolds also lays claim to that particular record. Buxton boasts a hot spring where no less than a quarter of a million gallons of water rise each day from a mile below ground at a constant temperature of 82° F. This also feeds the local swimming pool.

From Buxton we take the A5004 north and at the junction with the A6 turn right towards Chapel-en-le-Frith. The town derives its name from the original 13th century church, which would then have stood on the edge of a forest – hence, en-le-Frith. From the A6 we turn left onto the A624, travelling north to Glossop. Situated on the edge of High Peak in the Peak District National Park, this highly attractive centre is just 12 miles from the city of Manchester.

In Glossop we turn right to pick up the A57 and enter the National Park

Right: In the village of Ashford-In-The Water, the Sheepbridge with its quaint stone pen.

62

Down in the valley below Wormhill. Spectacular to say the least, but oh for a little sunshine to bring it all to life.

run alongside Ladybower for a couple of miles before turning right onto the A6013 where the road follows the side of the reservoir for another mile or so.

Just after the village of Bamford we turn right, picking up the A625 to make our way to the attractive little hamlet of Castleton.

Hard hat country

Around Castleton we find three or four fascinating caves. All are worth a visit. We picked Speedwell Cavern, which you will find at the foot of the spectacular Winnats Pass, high above Castleton.

Over 500 feet below the surface of the hill, the boat glides through the workings of a 200-year-old lead mine, which opens into a network of natural cave and underground rivers. Finally, you enter a magnificent cathedral-like cavern containing the awesome Bottomless Pit – a huge subterranean lake. The hard hats were an absolute must as during both the outward and return journeys on the boat, my head was constantly hitting the tunnel roof.

Back to the surface, it's time to move on, although you might want to visit one of the other well-known caverns in the area, the Blue John Cavern. It is here that the Blue John stone, a beautiful and ornamental fluor-spar, is mined. There are regular tours of the cavern and mine workings, which we recommend.

We leave Speedwell Cavern, driving up the hill and over the impressive Winnats Pass and then take the secondary road towards the village of Sparrowpit. Here we turn left onto the A623 following the attractive road for four or five miles. Keep an eye open for the B6521 and turn left into Eyam.

One of the largest and most pleasant Peak District villages, Eyam has a darker claim to fame. Set 800 feet up among the peaks, during the 17th century it was remote and isolated. However, its isolation could not protect it from the plague that was decimating the population of London. In 1665 a box of clothing containing plague germs was sent from London to George Vicars, Eyam tailor, who became infected and quickly died. The infection spread rapidly, and many of the villagers prepared to leave. But William Mompesson, the local rector, persuaded them to stay, in an effort to prevent the disease spreading to the surrounding villages. Out of an estimated population of 350 some 250 died, including Mompesson's wife. A high price to pay for their self-sacrifice.

63

ENJOYING YOUR JAGUAR

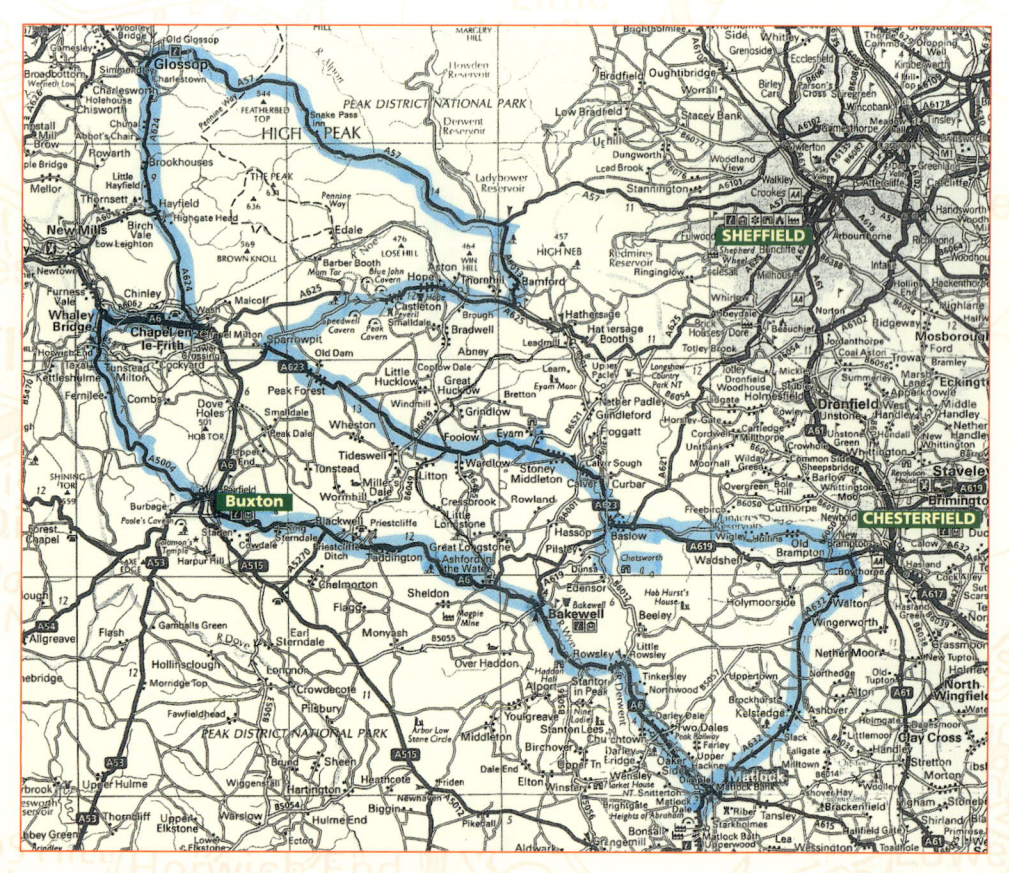

Stately home

Return to the A623 and turn left in the direction of Chesterfield. Just before we reach Baslow, we turn right onto the A619 and follow the signposts to Chatsworth House.

The home of the Duke and Duchess of Devonshire, this majestic property has been the family home for 450 years. Often referred to as a treasure house, each room is filled with the most exquisite furniture, porcelain and pictures. The grounds are equally stunning, with the much-photographed cascade waterfall forming a central feature. During the past five years, Chatsworth has been twice-voted the country's favourite national treasure in the NPI Gold Awards.

We return northbound on to the A623 and turn right to our next destination, the village of Baslow. Here you will find an ancient packhorse bridge that crosses the river Derwent leading to the greystone cottages and riverside parish church. At the far end of the bridge stands a stone-built toll-house that is thought to be the smallest in England. The church of St Anne's is worth a look; it's mostly 14th century with a 13th century tower and spire. In the porch you will find parts of a Saxon cross, and just inside the door a dog-whip, once used to drive away unruly dogs from the church. Goose Green in another part of the village is particularly attractive, with thatched cottages and a sparkling stream.

We now pick up the A619 east, about a mile further on turn left onto the B6050, and then right at an unclassified road driving through Wigley, Hollins and into the village of Old Brampton. If you've got a bit of time on your hands, try looking at the face of the clock on the south side of the church tower - it has 63 minutes marked on it!

The story goes that a craftsman employed to paint the face imbibed

64

Two classics together. Parked outside the Georgian Opera House in Buxton, the XKR was capable of making its own sweet music.

rather more than was good for him during a lunchtime break. Upon his return he was a little over enthusiastic with his counting and as result there are seven divisions between I and II, four between IV and V, six between VII and VIII, and six between X and XI.

We continue driving, through Old Brampton and at the crossroads turn right onto the B6050. From there we turn left to take the A619 towards the outskirts of Chesterfield, at which point we turn right and take the A632, driving onto the town of Matlock.

This busy town is the administrative centre of Derbyshire, and was once noted for its many imposing 'Hydros' or water temples of a healing nature. Today, these 'temples' are all history, but there are still many places of interest, and visiting all the town has to offer can easily fill a day.

Riber Castle should certainly be on the list. It dominates the countryside around Matlock. Perched on a hill 600 feet above the town, it looks most forbidding and would not be out of place in a horror movie. Designed and built by John Smedley in 1862 the castle remained derelict for many years until, in the 1960s, a group of zoologists set up a Nature Reserve for British and European Fauna. The castle is well worth a visit. especially for the views of the surrounding area.

Just a short drive south of the town, via a great natural gorge you will find Matlock Bath. High Tor, a massive limestone cliff towers 389ft above Matlock Dale and the River Derwent.

Opposite High Tor, separated only by the gorge, is the 1,100ft limestone mass of Massons Hill, the southern tip of which is known as the Heights of Abraham and descends sharply into Matlock Bath through a forest of trees. The woodland paths through the trees provide some striking views of Matlock Bath and the countryside beyond, although access is possible by cable car.

From Matlock we pick up the main A6 and head north west to another prominent Peak District town, Bakewell. Perhaps best known for its Bakewell Puddings (don't even think about calling them 'tarts' in this part of the country) the flaky almond confection was invented here around

Speedwell Cavern gift shop where jewellery and gifts are made from the 'Blue John' stones mined nearby.

ENJOYING YOUR JAGUAR

Just a corner of the wonderful Pavilion Gardens in the heart of Buxton.

Driving through the charming village of Ashford-In-The-Water.

Places of Interest

Speedwell Cavern
Apr-Oct 9.30am - 5.30pm
Nov-Mar 10.00am - 5.00pm

Blue John Cavern
Summer 9.30am - 5.30pm Winter 9.30am - Dusk

Chatsworth House
All Year 11.00am - 4.30pm

Riber Castle Wildlife Park
Open All Year

Haddon Hall
Apr-Sept 10.30am - 5.00pm Daily.
Oct Mon-Thur till 4.30pm

1860 when by mistake a cook poured egg on to the jam instead of the pastry.

The Romans settled here for the warm springs followed by the Saxons who named it 'Bad Quell' or 'bath well'. Most of the buildings date from the 17th and 18th centuries with the notable exception of the Old House Museum with its wattle and daub construction, which is at least 100 years older.

Journey's end

From Bakewell we complete our round trip with a look at another particularly attractive village. Tucked away just off the A6, one and half-miles north west of Bakewell you'll find Ashford-In-The-Water. The River Wye meanders through this little limestone village with its narrow streets and three ancient bridges. The 17th century Sheepwash Bridge has a stone enclosure at one end that was used to pen sheep prior to washing them in the river.

Behind Holy Trinity church are traces of a moat, all that remains of a fortified house which was the home of Edmund Plantagenet, brother of Edward II.

During our walk around the village we reach a particularly pleasant hotel. The Riverside Country House hotel appeared to be extremely comfortable and is one we shall certainly try when we are next in the area.

Rejoining the A6, it's only about eight-miles back to our start point in Buxton, although there is still one place not to be missed.

Lying just one and half-miles south of Buxton on the A6, you will find Haddon Hall, the most complete surviving Medieval Manor House in England. Built over a period of 400 years, it has been the home of the manners family for over 800 years.

Our mini tour concludes with the short drive back to Buxton.

The Hotels

The Palace Hotel
Buxton   01298 22001

Riverside Country House Hotel
Ashford-In-The-Water
01629 814275

The Villages

Castleton
Eyam
Baslow
Old Brampton
Ashford-In-The-Water

66